MAYA CALENDAR

VOICE OF THE GALAXY

RAYMOND MARDYKS
STACIA ALANA-LEAH

STAR HEART PUBLICATIONS
SEDONA, ARIZONA

ISBN 0-9644180-2-9

Star Heart Publications
P.O. Box 2841 Sedona, AZ 86339
starheart@sedona.net

TABLE OF CONTENTS

WELCOME

Many of us are experiencing a transformation and a major shift in consciousness at this time. This book, *Maya Calendar, Voice of the Galaxy* is here to assist us. It is a guide for being with what is happening in a more conscious way. Twenty archetypes, called "Daykeepers," are introduced in this book. The twenty day-signs of the Maya calendar represent these twenty archetypes.

The purpose of *Maya Calendar, Voice of the Galaxy,* is to bridge the levels of consciousness between the Daykeepers and human awareness. To access the deeper levels of the Maya calendar and Maya astrology, it is necessary to become intimate with the Daykeepers. The information in this book was inspired by working directly with these twenty archetypes.

The Daykeepers are archetypal beings. This means that they originate from beyond time and space as we understand it. The Daykeepers can be found just beyond the boundaries of our individual egos, just beyond the atmosphere of the planet Earth and just beyond the boundary of our solar system.

For an individual, the Daykeepers can assist the ego and personality to work more closely with the soul. For both the planet and the solar system, they are the guides to galactic consciousness. They welcome us to be more conscious participants in the Galaxy of which we, humanity, the Earth and the Sun are all a part.

As humanity evolves into a galactic race, we will need to use and access galactic time. This is a time beyond the movement of planets. It is a time that is created by the movement of the Daykeepers. ★

INTRODUCTION

What is the Maya calendar and what significance does it have for the rest of humanity? What is popularly referred to as the Maya calendar is actually a variety of many different calendars. These can all be recognized as parts of an advanced astrological system. The mathematical and astronomical calculations of the ancient Maya were far more accurate and sophisticated than that of any contemporary culture. Only in recent years has modern astronomy matched the precision of the Maya system.

Tzol'Kin is one name for the Maya's most sacred calendar. The Tzol'Kin can be used as a perpetual calendar that counts 260 days. There are two smaller cycles that make up this 260-day cycle. One is a thirteen-day cycle and the other is the twenty-day cycle of the Daykeepers. Each day of the Tzol'Kin is identified by a number from one to thirteen and one of the twenty Daykeepers. This allows thirteen times twenty (13 x 20), or 260 possible combinations.

The indigenous people of Mexico and Central America have passed on the Tzol'Kin count from the time of their earliest memories. Only a few of those involved with the calendar are able to carry this sacred knowledge to the level of recognizing the presence of the Daykeepers, known to them as the "Day Lords." These initiated shamans have taken on the responsibility of being human "daykeepers." Even to this day, they are sought after for their ability to bridge the gap between the invisible realms of the Daykeepers and the more familiar dimensions of our physical world.

These human daykeepers are often needed for their ability to assist in healing rituals. This includes finding the archetypal Daykeeper that can assist with an illness or problem. It is often believed that the problem or sickness is caused by a disconnection to, or the dishonoring of, one or more of the twenty Daykeepers. The human daykeeper bridges the gap and assists in reconnecting the ill human with the appropriate archetypal Daykeeper. When this is done, weaknesses are strengthened and illnesses can be healed. These healing rituals usually require making offerings to the Daykeepers.

What is unique about both the Tzol'Kin and Maya astrology is that they access the cycles that exist beyond the planets of our solar system. They access the galactic cycles which influence and affect the cycles of our solar system. To work intimately with the Tzol'Kin or Maya astrology, it is not only necessary to understand cycles of time, but also the *archetypal presence* within each cycle. Just like shamans acknowledge spirits and astrologers recognize the influence of signs and planets, human daykeepers and advanced Maya astrologers can recognize the presence and influence of the archetypal Daykeepers.

To become a human daykeeper, or to work with Maya astrology on a galactic level, you must be open to, and follow the guidance of, your Daykeeper. This is the Daykeeper of the day you were born. The next step would be to acknowledge and follow the 20-day (Imix to Ahaw) cycles and then the 13-day cycles. The thirteen numbers can be recognized as levels of the galactic tide, one being the lowest tide and thirteen being the highest.

Becoming intimate with the Daykeepers, and learning to recognize their presence, greatly shifts human consciousness. The Daykeepers cannot be accessed directly from within the limitations of the human ego. Following the Maya calendar is a journey. It is a gradual process of expanding consciousness beyond the personality, which is solar-system based, and into true time, which is galactic.

It is recommended that you approach the Daykeepers with few expectations and an open heart. The Daykeepers reveal their presence in a multitude of ways. To consistently access their presence directly, you must be able to easily shift out of your ego and expand your consciousness.

True time, or galactic time, is a level of movement and a frequency. To live consciously in galactic time, you must first become a whole and integrated ego. This creates a vessel in which the soul can be present. Galactic time may be accessed only when a certain level of consciousness has been obtained.

When egos are fragmented, as much of humanity's egos are, they cannot carry the fluid of the soul. The soul is an expanded consciousness that is not restricted to the human body. It is a dimension of your galactic, higher self that already exists in true time. Once your ego is balanced and integrated, you can consciously participate with your soul's work.

Galactic time is accessible only to humans who have evolved beyond fear and fragmentation. For you to move from fragmentation to wholeness, you must first release all judgment. Then without judgment, you must take responsibility for all that you experience. This is absolutely necessary for you to evolve into your galactic potential.

Both the Tzol'Kin and Maya astrology hold a key to accessing the galactic level of self, by accessing galactic time. When the Maya calendar is worked with in the proper way, it can harmonize and tune the human form and consciousness to the galactic "tone." This galactic tone is a voice of the Galaxy. Nearly all of humanity experiences this tone as fragmented.

On different levels, the human ego and the solar system act as filters. They both fragment the one tone into many. The twenty Daykeepers carry the fragmented pieces of the one galactic tone. By working with the Daykeepers and becoming familiar with them, you are guided back to the original one tone.

The Daykeepers are essentially the voice of the Galaxy. They are the voice that reaches humanity and touches our consciousness. We are now being invited to become more intimate with the Daykeepers. We can do this by acknowledging their presence and expanding our human awareness to include the galactic voice.

The Daykeepers have returned at this time because it is necessary for humanity to access true time. The "Galactic Wave" is encompassing our entire solar system, including the Earth. It will wash out the memories of civilization as we know it to be. True time will resume for us, as it was for the ancestors who seeded humanity on this planet in the beginning of the illusion of time. ★

SUGGESTIONS

An oracle is a medium through which you may receive communications from the spirit world. The beings accessible through the ritual use of the Tzol'Kin calendar are the twenty Daykeepers, who are symbolized by twenty day-signs. Working with symbols and interacting consciously with the beings these symbols represent are two very different experiences.

The information in this book about each Daykeeper originates directly from the Daykeepers themselves. The Daykeepers have asked that this information be shared and made accessible to humanity. It is time for us to consciously evolve into a galactic race that uses galactic time. Time is a multidimensional experience. There are many levels of time that can be acknowledged as true time, depending on the focus and location of your consciousness. If you stay conscious of only the passage of days, based the Earth's movement along its axis and around the Sun, then your consciousness remains on the Earth.

The Tzol'Kin represents a galactic passage of time. If you are initiated by the Daykeepers, then your consciousness may exceed the Earthly plane, into the realms of the Galaxy. The Daykeepers have been used by the native people of Mexico and Central America as a means of maintaining the galactic time they kept before entering their Earthly form. This unique key to accessing your galactic, higher self is now available to all who recognize and acknowledge its sacredness.

The most important aspect of working with the Tzol'Kin is the ability to recognize the Daykeepers. There is a quality of presence that each Daykeeper reveals. The ability to recognize this presence in your life enables you to acknowledge the presence of galactic time and evolve into a more conscious, galactic citizen. The techniques offered in this chapter open the door to consciously acknowledging and accessing the presence of the Daykeepers.

DIVINATION

STEP 1.
Hold in your thoughts a picture of what you want the Daykeepers to help you with. Arrive into your heart center and open your heart. Ask the Daykeepers, from your heart center, which of them can assist you with this.

STEP 2.
Close your eyes and visualize the Daykeepers. Stay present in your heart and allow your intuition to guide you to a number from one to twenty. Then look up the Daykeeper on the key page (p. 14) and open to its chapter in this book.

STEP 3.
Read the information that you feel in your heart to read. Open to the message of the words and allow yourself to experience the presence of the Daykeeper.

While acknowledging the presence of the Daykeeper and the qualities experienced in its presence, expand beyond your normal state of consciousness. Continue to allow your consciousness to expand and include a higher level of who you are to participate in your personal life. ★

DAILY RITUAL

To become more familiar with the presence of the Daykeepers, you may choose to open yourself to the Daykeeper of each day. For example, on the first day of each 20-day cycle, it is the day of Imix. You may open to the Imix chapter and read what your heart draws you to or guides you to read. Open your heart and feel the Daykeeper's presence. It is necessary to maintain an open heart to consciously access the their presence. On the next day you may want to open yourself to Ik, and so on. After the twenty-day cycle is complete, you may choose to begin again with Imix.

This can be done as a ritual meditation to bring in the new Daykeeper for each day. The Tzol'Kin day begins and ends at sunset. This is when one Daykeeper completes its day and the new Daykeeper arrives.

Every day at sunset, you may meditate with an image of the new Daykeeper in your mind. Open your heart and welcome in the new day. Read from the Daykeeper's chapter and recognize its presence throughout the rest of its day. As sunset approaches, feel the completion of the day.

Presently there are two Tzol'Kin counts in popular use. This is discussed in more detail later on in this book. These counts offer two different Daykeepers for each day. You may choose to acknowledge the presence of one or both of these Daykeepers. To find the Daykeeper for each day, you can use the **Daykeeper Finder** located near the back of this book. ★

DAYKEEPER BIRTH SIGN

Find the Daykeeper for the day of your birth by using the **Daykeeper Finder**. Using the Traditional count, the New Age count or both, turn to the Daykeeper chapter. It is important to recognize that the Daykeeper is a guide to a more expanded state of consciousness, what can be considered galactic consciousness. You may or may not have the immediate experience of identifying with your Daykeeper.

The Daykeeper for the day of your birth is significant. It is the guide that directly accesses you to your life responsibilities. You may find other Daykeepers have an equally significant impact on your life. They may appear to be more significant than the Daykeeper for your birth. Either way, the Daykeeper for your birth can ground you into your life responsibilities and awaken you to the deeper meaning and purpose in your life.

Meditate with your birth Daykeeper. The more resistance that you encounter with this Daykeeper, the more beneficial it will be for you to open to it and have a more conscious and expanded experience of it. ★

DAYKEEPER KEY PAGE

1. IMIX
ONE, ORIGINAL, SOURCE

2. IK
BREATH, EXPANSION, RELEASE

3. AK'BAL
EQUALITY, HARMONY, DAWN

4. K'AN
ACTIVATE, PREPARE, INVEST

5. CHIK'CHAN
SIMPLE, NATURAL, INSTINCT

6. KIMI
DEATH, ETERNAL, ANCESTOR

7. MANIK
ACCOMPLISH, POTENTIAL, FUTURE

8. LAMAT
REPRODUCE, MULTIPLY, GROW

9. MULUK
INTERDEPENDENT, RELIABLE, DUTY

10. OK
IMPULSIVE, SENSUAL, DESIRE

11. CHUEN
ENJOY, CREATE, UNITE

12. EB
GUIDE, DESTINY, PATH

13. BEN
DEPENDENT, FAMILY, SUPPORT

14. IX
INDIVIDUAL, SPIRIT, FREEDOM

15. MEN
ENVISION, FOCUS, PRODUCE

16. KIB
ALONE, SEPARATE, SOLITARY

17. KABAN
MIND, THOUGHT, EVOLUTION

18. ETZ'NAB
DIVIDE, SACRIFICE, CHANGE

19. KAWAK
SUDDEN, UNEXPECTED, SHIFT

20. AHAW
ENCOMPASS, COMPLETE, END

The new spellings of the Daykeeper names reflect recent developments in the Mayan alphabet. These make the names easier to pronounce: "a" sounds like "a" in father; "e" sounds like "e" in pet; "i" sounds like "ee" in beet; "u" sounds like "oo" in boot and "x" sounds like "sh" in push.

THE DAYKEEPERS

IMIX

TRADITIONAL: Alligator or Crocodile
DREAMSPELL: Red Dragon
KICHÉ: Imosh

ICON: The round form near the top of the icon symbolizes oneness. The circles around this represent the seeds or children of the oneness. The lines near the bottom represent the growth that arises from the seeds of the oneness.

ESSENCE: Imix is the beginning of a cycle. It is the fragmentation of the one, in order to create many. This fragmentation or offspring of the one still carries the essence of the original source. Everything is one. Imix is the essence of oneness within all things.

SYMBOL: The crocodile is an ancient inhabitant of the Earth. It is a pure representation of a primordial ancestor, which remains on the Earth today, unchanged from its prehistoric form. It has chosen not to evolve out of or abandon its watery origins. It maintains an almost constant connection to the water, remaining true to the source of its life.

MANIFESTATIONS: Imix often manifests in human reality as the ability to remain in the present moment without concern for the past or future. It can be recognized as a clear link to that which lies beyond the mundane. Imix offers the ability to transcend time and to refrain from having time-oriented desires.

On an Imix day, you may want to be less structured. Make time for yourself that is free from previous commitments and obligations. This is an opportune day to discover from within what you really want and where you truly want to go in your life. It is a day to acknowledge that which lies beyond time.

People who are born on an Imix day are often dreamers that lack the desire to succeed in more materialistic accomplishments. They often come up with the new ideas that others bring into manifestation.

KEY WORDS: begin, dreamer, new, oneness, original, root and source.

Imix essentially represents the original source from which all known things come. By working with Imix, you can access this source within everything. Imix will guide you deeper in, where you have the potential to transcend duality and be in a peaceful state of oneness with everything. With Imix, you must release all judgment and limitations. To work consciously with this Daykeeper is to be present in your center, allowing the true desires and the greatest potential to manifest through and from that center.

MEDITATION FOR IMIX

Focus on the image of Imix, either in your mind or on the icon before you. Release all tension. Breathe yourself into a more relaxed and open state. Focus on the round object at the top of the icon. Find the place within yourself that resonates with this image. Hold your consciousness here and allow all images and thoughts to simply be released. Your conscious connection to your origin is in this place within you. It is this place in consciousness that allows and enables you to access all that originates from the same source. Once you are able to achieve clarity within this space, observe the energy emanating from this here. It is constantly creating new life through you. When you are able to observe this process within yourself without attempting to manipulate or control it, then you are consciously embodying Imix.

As you begin to master the ability to recognize Imix within this creative process, you can begin to recognize this quality that is within everything and everyone. The more easily this process flows within you, the more easily you recognize this process within others. You may then obtain a blissful state of being while Imix is activated. You may find your consciousness shift into a more accepting and peaceful state. The key to successfully integrating and embodying Imix is to continually release all judgments. Judgment creates the illusion of separation and keeps you from accessing this place of origin that emanates from within everyone and everything.

NOTES AND INSIGHTS:

IK

TRADITIONAL: Wind
DREAMSPELL: White Wind
KICHÉ: Iq'

ICON: The circle in the center represents the source of the wind. It is divided to symbolize the balance of masculine and feminine within the source. The two lines coming from the center represent the movement of the wind in two different directions, eventually returning to its place of origin.

ESSENCE: Ik is the expansion and bursting out of new life, like a seed sprouting through its shell. It expands boundaries, just as an inhalation of breath expands the size of the lungs. It is the spirit which thrusts itself out of form and travels with the wind, like pollen traveling from flower to flower.

SYMBOL: The wind represents a presence from far away. It can be a carrier of a message or a destructive force that can knock down certain boundaries.

MANIFESTATIONS: Ik can manifest in the human experience as impulses, actions or behaviors that seem out of character or out of control.

Ik days provide an opportunity to push beyond your accepted beliefs or those of society. It is a day for revelations and the realization that there is more that exists beyond the boundaries we create. Expand your boundary voluntarily and be open to new possibilities and unexpected opportunities. Consider doing something different or unusual for who you believe yourself to be.

Those born on an Ik day bring influences from outside to their group or family that stimulate growth in new directions.

KEY WORDS: air, anger, breath, burst, expansion, flood, frenzy, fury, hatred, landslide, release, strong, violent, violent rainstorms and wild.

Ik manifests as something that has penetrated your boundary by force. It brings with it the opportunity to experience something unknown. Ik also offers the opportunity to reconstruct your boundaries to include more of who you are. Ik can be perceived as a violent intrusion or an exciting transformation. This often depends on the perception and openness of the person who encounters Ik.

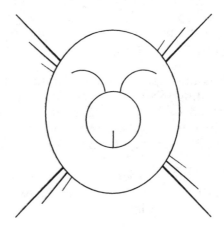

MEDITATION FOR IK

Focus on the image of Ik, either in your mind or on the icon. Welcome Ik's presence with a deep inhalation. Release all tension and breathe yourself into a more relaxed and open state. Focus on the image of the wind that escapes in separate directions from the center. Allow your consciousness to travel with the wind. Observe its movements and flow without attempting to manipulate or control it. Watch where the wind takes your consciousness.

Allow the wind to clear your consciousness and break down unnecessary barriers that no longer serve a positive purpose for you. Observe the seeds of new life, the new thoughts and new ideas that travel with the wind. Observe that your consciousness, traveling with the wind, is a new life, with new thoughts and ideas, and has penetrated into an unfamiliar place.

Ik carries consciousness to unexplored territory. Each individual is both the new territory as well as the new ideas. There is a constant motion and flow to each journey; each point along the journey is a center, reaching out in separate directions to encircle all that is and return to its point of origin.

To consciously work with and embody Ik's essence, you must allow your consciousness to easily move through and beyond all boundaries. It takes practice and a commitment to trust and honor the sacred path of the wind. You must be willing to allow the natural flow of the thought process to occur without any interference. This requires giving up the illusion of control and releasing all expectations. It takes a commitment to finding the present moment and allowing your consciousness to be present in the moment. The present moment is traveling on the wind, like your consciousness, in separate directions. Your consciousness must be fluid and detached to be present in the moment. This is Ik's gift to you.

NOTES AND INSIGHTS:

AK'BAL

TRADITIONAL: Dawn, House or Night
DREAMSPELL: Blue Night
KICHÉ: Aq'abal

ICON: The two forms coming from the sides of the icon represent light and darkness or mother and father. The triangle between them represents the shared space where they merge together equally as one. The three mountains represent the horizon, or a trinity such as mother, father and child.

ESSENCE: Ak'bal is the dawning of a new light. It is the continuous coming together of the old and the new to create a new day, a new light and a new force. Somewhere on the Earth, a new day is always dawning.

SYMBOL: Ak'bal is symbolized by the dawn, by the meeting of the light and the darkness. It is the equal expression of the two, united together as one.

MANIFESTATIONS: Ak'bal manifests as a completion and the natural beginning that immediately follows. Ak'bal's presence is like a mystery being revealed. It happens only after something else, something necessary, happens first. Ak'bal guides what and when something is revealed, as it comes to light out of the darkness or to consciousness from the unconscious.

Ak'bal's day is for revelations and for the next generation's truths to manifest. Be open to new messages or information appropriate for the immediate present or future, but not for the past.

Those who are born on an Ak'bal day are dreamers and visionaries. They desire to bring forth something new in the natural evolution of what is becoming outdated or complete.

KEY WORDS: aurora, coupling, day and night, dawn, dreams, equality, harmony, intuition, light and dark, marriage, meeting place, psychologist, spring equinox, two-sided and united.

Ak'bal remains, with an ever-present awareness of light and dark, in the place where these two forces merge. This is a creative and destructive place. Ak'bal is a step beyond duality, and its presence often forces you to come out of the extreme light or dark into a mutual place of consciousness.

MEDITATION FOR AK'BAL

Focus on the image of Ak'bal, either in your mind or on the icon before you. Relax, release all tension and breathe yourself into a more relaxed state. Focus on the center of the image and allow your consciousness to be drawn into this neutral space. While in this space be aware of a light that brilliantly shines and warms and penetrates this space from your right. Be aware of a still, quiet darkness that cools and penetrates the neutral space from your left. Allow these apparent opposing forces to merge in the neutral space that your consciousness occupies.

Observe how these forces merge without any attempt to manipulate or control them in any way. Allow for a natural balance to occur within yourself. Release any boundaries or barricades that prevent this.

The key to working consciously with Ak'bal is to open your mind and heart to the creative and destructive forces at play. Maintain your conscious center within a neutral and balanced place. Release expectations and allow for all possibilities to exist at once. Ak'bal manifests often as an opposing force that ultimately balances. By releasing set agendas and opening to this new input, you can experience a greater potential of the moment and become an equal participant with the creative forces that shape reality as we know it.

The greatest potential of Ak'bal comes with the invitation and the possibility of expanding consciousness to encompass the light, the dark and the neutral or gray space where the light and dark merge. This is represented by the three mountainlike shapes on the horizon.

To work consciously with Ak'bal, you must practice expanding consciousness with an open mind and continue to release all expectations and all agendas. You must proceed with the understanding that everything is equal and all opposition is valid. Ak'bal incorporates and manifests through the three dimensions that create reality as we know it.

NOTES AND INSIGHTS:

K'AN

TRADITIONAL: Lizard, Net or Seed
DREAMSPELL: Yellow Seed
KICHÉ: K'at

ICON: The round object near the top of the icon represents a seed with the potential for new life. The horizontal line below this represents a net or the Earth prepared for receiving the seed. The vertical lines along the bottom of the icon represent the source of nourishment for the new life within the seed. These lines also suggest what is being filtered through the net.

ESSENCE: K'an is instinctual, primal wholeness. Contained within the simplest of forms, it carries the potential to ignite the growth of new life. K'an is also the fire within the heart.

SYMBOL: The seed symbolizes the potential for new life. K'an is also sometimes represented by a net. This symbolizes a filtering that separates the old from the new. The net may also carry the seed and assist it in finding a place to begin its new life.

MANIFESTATIONS: K'an manifests as an apparently destructive force that eliminates or destroys what is complete. An example of this is a burning forest that allows for new life to begin there. K'an is also the feeding or fueling of this new life.

A K'an day is a good time to support and encourage new ideas or plans, though they may not yet be recognized by others and may not be ready to be acted on.

Those born on this day may carry or reflect the potential of future accomplishments.

KEY WORDS: activate, awaken, burn, discipline, engage, fire, heart energy, ignite, initiate, instigate, invest, planting,, potential, prepare, seed money and stimulate.

K'an ignites the spark of new life. It is embodied within the seed that has the potential to grow into a living, evolving thing. K'an also rejects that which is not ready or not appropriate for becoming enriched with life. K'an extends beyond the seed to the entire system. It chooses what is appropriate for new life and what must be destroyed for this new life to flourish.

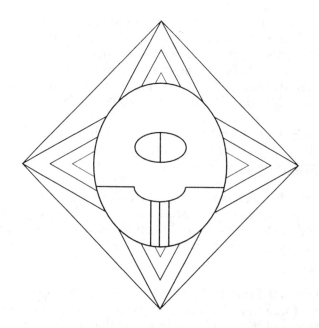

MEDITATION FOR K'AN

Relax and focus on the image of K'an, either on the icon before you or in your mind. Open your heart and breathe yourself into a more relaxed state. Focus on your heart center. The heart sends potential seeds of nourishment, in the form of oxygen, throughout your physical body. These seeds are implanted and received where they are needed within your physical body. Be aware that there is a natural filtering system within you. You will find that K'an's presence will ground you into your physical body and make this filtering, feeding and growth process more conscious and deliberate.

You are capable of participating more consciously in this process by quietly observing K'an's presence within your reality. Watch the desire to seize control over this process and let it dissolve. Let the "net" filter out what is unnecessary and an obstacle for life and evolution. You are the net, you are the seed and you are the warm, nurturing love that ignites the seed and awakens new life. All of these are aspects of who you are. Allow them to work through you and with you in a divine and sacred way that allows the highest evolution for everyone and everything.

To more consciously work with K'an, you must release expectations and be open to new ideas of what is appropriate for embodying life and evolution. Things that have become extinct are no longer appropriate vessels for the energy and frequencies that we experience as life. This is a decision made by life itself and should not be challenged or regretted, but celebrated as the gift of evolution. The system that filters the dead from the living is a system of destruction and life. These two work together to create reality as we know it. Each step in the process is ultimately a natural step toward a more evolved state and a more evolved reality. This process can be observed, it can be celebrated, but it cannot be tampered with. It encompasses and includes everything, living or dead.

NOTES AND INSIGHTS:

CHIK'CHAN

TRADITIONAL: Serpent
DREAMSPELL: Red Serpent
KICHÉ: Kan

ICON: The grid near the top of the icon represents the deep, inner back area of the brain, which is highly intuitive. The circles coming out of this represent the fragmenting of the intuitive nature. The nose and mouth represent the deeper, instinctual and often more reliable senses of smell and taste.

ESSENCE: Chik'chan is the natural flow. It is the simplicity of the primal nature within everything. It is instinctual and intuitive knowing, unchanged by human reasoning.

SYMBOL: The snake represents and carries a primal, instinctual recognition and understanding. This awareness is filtered through human consciousness, fragmenting the primal knowledge.

MANIFESTATIONS: Chik'chan's presence may be experienced as a sensitivity to nature in its simplicity. With this comes an ability to correct what has been altered from its natural state. This is done to return to a relaxed state of being. Your conscious awareness is then clear and uncomplicated.

Chik'chan days are good for accessing the deeper instincts of human nature. Try doing something with your eyes closed or in the dark. Distinguish between the fears that genuinely warn you of danger and those that complicate your life and keep you from trusting your true desires.

Those born with Chik'chan as their Daykeeper have a sensitivity to the simplicity within all things. They possess the ability to realign with the natural flow. This can be done for themselves as well as for others. They have the potential of being a healer when this ability is trusted and developed.

KEY WORDS: curing, foundation, fear, healing, instinct, intuition, medicine, natural, protection, reptilian, serpent and simple.

Chik'chan is an independent source of intuition and discernment. Chik'chan embodies and relies upon a basic deep inner knowing that is inherent within every sentient being. The ability to trust this inner instinct is not always accessible to individuals, as much of humanity relies on what could be considered false senses to create their experience of reality.

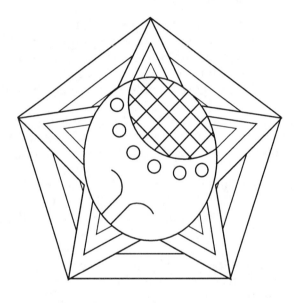

MEDITATION FOR CHIK'CHAN

Relax and focus on the image of Chik'chan. Close your eyes and hold the image in your consciousness. Breathe yourself into a more relaxed state. Allow your consciousness to remain centered in the back area of your brain. Feel a warmth emanating from this place. Allow this warmth to spread throughout the rest of your body.

Observe the shift in consciousness that is created while you are focused in this center. As long as you allow this to be the center and focus of your consciousness, you are accessing a deeper intuition and a more relaxed way of being.

Envision the Serpent and become aware of the Serpent's ability to create its experience of reality by relying on the deeper senses of smell and taste. It is not necessary for the Serpent to hear or see. The senses of sight and hearing can trick you into believing in an illusion. They fragment and distort the deeper intuitive sense and understanding that is within each of us. It can be very beneficial to access this area in the back of the brain directly and allow a deeper, truer sense of what is real to unfold before you.

Chik'chan can guide you into a more open and trusting state by assisting in the process of observing illusions and releasing expectations of reality. This is a gift given to humanity and all sentient beings by the Serpent. It is a gift of truth and the ability to perceive it. To work consciously with Chik'chan, you must be willing to release all expectations of what reality is and what creates it. You must be willing to go into the darkness and into the silence to reclaim a deeper understanding of your own intuition. Take all troubles or problems to this center in the back of your brain and perceive them from here, in the quiet darkness. By doing this, you allow these so-called problems to be perceived and recognized for what they truly are – a gift.

NOTES AND INSIGHTS:

KIMI

TRADITIONAL: Death or Skull
DREAMSPELL: White World-Bridger
KICHÉ: Kamé

ICON: The eye on the face of the icon is closed to represent the sleep of death. The jaw represents an opening into the individual's soul. The teeth carry the potential of the individual from his/her ancestry through future generations.

ESSENCE: Kimi is the completion of life, as humans know it, in a physical vessel or body. Kimi encompasses the mysteries of death.

SYMBOL: The skull symbolizes what is left behind after death. It represents what is human and cannot be easily destroyed. What the skull symbolizes remains forever available to future generations.

MANIFESTATIONS: Those affected by Kimi's presence may be aware of ancestors, both their own and those of others. Kimi may bring to your awareness the immortal spirit within and beyond the human body.

On Kimi days, you may choose to remember your ancestors, appreciate what has been passed on to you and remember that a part of you lives on forever.

Those born with Kimi as their Daykeeper are capable of clarifying the meaning and purpose of death through discovering the gifts of humanity's ancestors. They respect those who have come before them and often give voice to those whose voices are no longer heard.

KEY WORDS: ancestor, archaeology, bones, cemetery, death, deceased, eternal, imperishable, inheritance, skull, shaman, skeleton and spirit.

Kimi manifests and embodies death as we know it. Death and destruction are not to be mistaken for each other. Death is a movement in a particular direction. It awakens your consciousness to limitlessness. Destruction destroys boundaries whereas death expands beyond them. Death is not necessarily a physical occurrence. It is a movement of spirit that usually occurs when a body dies, but it can also happen while the body still lives. Small deaths occur from moment to moment. A more complete death occurs when your idea of who you are, and what reality is, is questioned and transformed.

Conscious death is a gift of transformation. It is a liberating experience that reconnects your conscious self with more complete and expanded levels of consciousness.

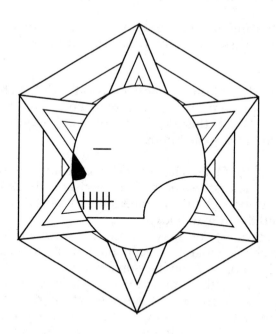

MEDITATION FOR KIMI

Relax and focus on the image of Kimi, either on the icon before you or in your mind. Breathe yourself into a more relaxed state. Focus your consciousness on the bones in your head. Your skull supports and protects. It is a perfect boundary and container for your consciousness. Open your mouth and observe the shift that this open and receptive position creates. This opening permits you to receive nourishment. It is important to recognize that death is also nourishment that promotes growth and expansion.

Fear is a boundary that we often become aware of when our consciousness is pushing through it. Allow the boundary to exist. Allow the fear to be a container in the same way that your skull is a container. Observe the opening in the fear and move through it. Your consciousness is fluid. It will continue to travel through openings and transform in relationship to the boundaries that contain it. Death is movement through the opening, beyond the former boundary. Recognize this process as sacred and receive it as a gift.

To work consciously with Kimi, you must recognize that the fear of death is simply an awareness that a change or transformation is occurring. Transformation is a necessary and constant companion of life. It feeds your soul and opens you to new possibilities. It is in this expanded state of awareness that you may recognize the presence of ancestors and future generations. These souls are the nourishment of life. They are the bond and channel to the essence of who we all are.

NOTES AND INSIGHTS:

MANIK

TRADITIONAL: Deer
DREAMSPELL: Blue Hand
KICHÉ: Kiej

ICON: The symbol of the hand represents the "tool" used for humanity's effect on the future. The position of the hand shows the unique feature of the human thumb. This characteristic allows humans to do things that no other animal can do. The hand is severed or detached to show both its potential and the loss of potential when handless.

ESSENCE: Manik carries the essence of evolution and growth toward something greater and more complete. Manik is what carries humanity into the future.

SYMBOL: The young deer represents the perfection of youth and the potential within youth for the future.

MANIFESTATIONS: Manik's presence may be experienced as a connection to the future. You may feel that what you are involved in is leading to something bigger or better.

Manik's day is good for preparing and being ready for what is still to come. You may need to trust the process and wait a while longer before realizing the outcome of your involvement and contribution.

Those born on a Manik day may experience a sense of being important for the future, being ahead of their time or carrying something for future generations.

KEY WORDS: accomplishment, blue, deer, domineering, evolution, fast, future, hand, manage, manipulate, permission, potential, powerful, prepare, prophecy and training.

Manik is both the tools necessary for creation and the potential of what is to be created. Manik offers an opportunity to observe possibilities as well as to bring these possibilities into manifestation. There are always many options and many possibilities, although the possibilities of manifestation are limited to what tools are available. Manik's presence includes a continuing evolution of the tools for manifesting or evolving possibilities.

MEDITATION FOR MANIK

Relax and focus on the image of Manik, either on the icon before you or in your mind. Breathe yourself into a more relaxed state. Notice the position of the hand. The thumb and the pointer touch. This creates an open, flowing channel throughout the hand.

Recognize that the hand is severed and separated from the body. This is to remind us that the tools we use for manifestation are gifts that are not to be taken for granted. Be aware that there are limitless possibilities and open yourself as a tool. Allow for the highest possibilities to manifest through you.

We each have a responsibility to continue the growth and evolution of humanity. Be aware that what you do and what you create will have a lasting impression on generations to come. With this awareness, create beauty that will nurture and sustain these future generations and contribute to a more loving and beautiful world for them to live in. Allow yourself to visualize and recognize what you can offer as an unconditional gift for the future of humanity.

To work consciously with Manik, you must transcend ego and find larger centers that include the rest of humanity, the rest of the world and the rest of the universe as we know it. By doing this, you can access a more evolved state of consciousness that will lead to an even more evolved state of consciousness. Future generations will continue on this journey.

Manik is not only the breakthrough concept or idea, it is the ability to actually break through one's former limitations to a new level of existence. This includes technology and science, among other things. Manik will lead your consciousness on an evolutionary journey and guide your hands to create a more evolved way of living and being.

NOTES AND INSIGHTS:

LAMAT

TRADITIONAL: Rabbit
DREAMSPELL: Yellow Star
KICHÉ: Q'anil

ICON: This image represents a division into four. The space in the middle of the icon represents the separation. The circle inside each of the four divisions represents the wholeness within each individual piece.

ESSENCE: Lamat's essence is the growth and reproductive stages of the creative process. It is the manifestation of the opportunity and potential contained within the seed.

SYMBOL: The rabbit symbolizes an ability to quickly reproduce and efficiently create new life at a rapid pace.

MANIFESTATIONS: Lamat's presence may be experienced as an inner awakening. It may be a new truth revealing itself and developing. Lamat can be a growth spurt, with a sudden movement or development toward success or completion.

When Lamat is the Daykeeper, you may find that certain activities move along more quickly and easily. These are good days for manifestation and for reproducing what has already been done.

Those born on a Lamat day may experience a new potential within themselves. It is an ability that appears to be unique or different from that of family members, friends and associates.

KEY WORDS: create, develop, duplicate, energy, growth, increase, life, multiply, rabbit, reproduction and ripen.

Lamat is separation that creates and promotes growth. It is like the division of cells that creates a new body. It is all that is involved in reproduction as we know it. Lamat's natural movement is separation and growth. Its purpose is to multiply.

MEDITATION FOR LAMAT

Relax and focus on the image of Lamat, either on the icon in front of you or in your mind. Breathe yourself into a more relaxed state. Observe how the icon represents one form separated into four forms. Each of these four forms is whole and complete, yet together they make one complete form. It is this movement of separation that creates growth on the physical level.

Visualize your body as one complete form. Allow your consciousness to travel into more microscopic levels of who you are. Observe the many small, yet complete objects or cells that make up your body. On this level, everything moves at a very rapid pace, efficiently working to create a larger body.

Allow your consciousness to return to your body as one form and then expand your vision outward to observe and recognize how your body is one small form in the body of the Earth. Allow your consciousness to expand even more to recognize that the Earth is one small form or body that lives within and cocreates this solar system. The pace of growth and movement is relative to where your consciousness is focused. When your consciousness travels to the inner, deeper microscopic world within, the growth process appears very rapid. When your consciousness travels to a more expanded and larger form or body, such as the Earth or the solar system, the movements and growth processes appear to be slower and slower.

To work consciously with Lamat, you must be willing to question your perception of time and movement. It is important to recognize the growth process inherent in all things. This process and its movement are what create your experience and perception of time and reality. Lamat can bridge many different levels of reality. You must be willing to release the expectations and perception of normal time to travel over these bridges and recognize your purpose from a different perspective.

NOTES AND INSIGHTS:

MULUK

TRADITIONAL: Rain or Water
DREAMSPELL: Red Moon
KICHÉ: Toj

ICON: The circle in the center of the icon represents a drop of water. It is one singular drop to show the simplicity of the source of life. The circle and surrounding components symbolize a continuing cycle, forever re-creating a singular drop of water.

ESSENCE: The essence of Muluk is interdependence and acknowledging the interconnection between all things.

SYMBOL: The rain represents what is carried in the air. This reveals the interdependency of oxygen and water and their on-going relationship.

MANIFESTATIONS: Your experience of Muluk may include feeling a sense of debt, a desire for unconditional giving or an unwillingness to give.

A day with Muluk as Daykeeper is a good time to consider what is needed to maintain productive and agreeable relationships. Demonstrate your appreciation and fulfill your obligations to those who support you.

Those born on a Muluk day must rely on others to fulfill certain responsibilities. They also need to be involved in the projects of others. They are often most successful as team players.

KEY WORDS: accounting, air, borrow, debt, duty, interdependence, mitigate, needy, obligation, payment, rain, reliable, remorse, repay, thunder and water.

Muluk connects two seemingly different worlds to create one larger world. This is represented by, and can be recognized in, the water cycle, where water is drawn from the Earth into the sky and returns to replenish the Earth. This interdependency creates a more nurturing and complete environment. Everything is connected. Everything is one.

MEDITATION FOR MULUK

Relax and focus on the image of Muluk, either on the icon before you or in your mind. Breathe yourself into a more relaxed state. Focus on the area around your navel and allow this to become a center for your consciousness. This area was once connected to a cord that bridged your small world in the womb to the larger world of your mother. Through this cord all nourishment was received. This is not the only cord that has connected you or presently connects you to something larger. There are also energetic cords that bridge the smaller world of your ego to the larger world of what can be considered your higher self.

Relax and visualize a single drop of water. Visualize its journey out of a larger body of water to be absorbed into the atmosphere to form a cloud with many other drops of water. Stay with the cloud in your mind and observe its journey through the atmosphere, receiving and pulling into it more drops of water. Observe the drop of water that you followed into the cloud as it is dropped and released back to the ground. Where does it land? Does it land on the Earth, in a puddle or in a large body of water? Following the path of a single drop of water could be an infinite journey. This is Muluk's message and gift – infinity.

Each of our souls is like a drop of water, constantly moving, constantly seeking out other souls to share a pool with. We drop into these human bodies and nourish them with new life. Just the awareness of the existence of the soul level of yourself bridges a smaller world and creates a larger one.

To work consciously with Muluk, you must open your consciousness to include the infinite journey that lives within each present moment. Muluk is a guide and is the essence within this eternal space. When you are conscious of eternity, you are conscious of Muluk's presence. The relationships among all interdependent things are constantly changing. To truly honor Muluk, you must trust and arrive in the moment. Recognize the sacredness of the moment and the sacredness of your surroundings. Falling into a pool of water is as sacred an experience as landing onto a barren desert. This is only one small step on the infinite journey.

NOTES AND INSIGHTS:

OK

TRADITIONAL: Dog
DREAMSPELL: White Dog
KICHÉ: Tzi'

ICON: The double-shaped brain near the center of the icon represents an evolved consciousness and a complex awareness. The two circles represent the ability to focus and perceive the complexity of this consciousness. The face represents the senses available for this consciousness.

ESSENCE: Ok is essentially animalistic desires. It is the simplicity and potency of desire. Ok is also the connection to inner knowing. It can be sensitivity to primal instincts as well as more evolved levels of intuition.

SYMBOL: The dog symbolizes a loyal and evolved animal that is attuned to its own desires, its surroundings and the desires of others. This includes sensitivity to human desires.

MANIFESTATIONS: Ok may be experienced as a heightened sensitivity to your inner feelings and desires, as well as enhanced awareness of your environment. Ok may express as strong desire, a sense of loyalty or the need to allow desire to guide your actions.

Ok's days are good for allowing yourself to be guided by your desires and intuition, trusting yourself and enjoying every moment.

Those born on an Ok day may be loyal, flamboyant, intuitive and available for the true desires of the moment.

KEY WORDS: complexity, desire, dog, faithful, guided, hungry, impulsive, initiation, intuition, loyalty, perceptive, scent, sensual, sexual, spontaneous and trust.

Ok embodies a level of consciousness that responds to the desires created through the senses. Ok is sensual awareness. This includes smell, sight, hearing and feeling. Ok acts immediately and spontaneously when senses are stimulated. There is also an ability to contemplate and consider the consequences of an action, although it is a simple desire that generally drives Ok and motivates its actions.

MEDITATION FOR OK

Focus on the image of Ok, either on the icon before you or in your mind. Relax and breathe yourself into a more relaxed state. Allow your consciousness to focus somewhere near the center of your brain. Experience this center as a clear and uncomplicated space that includes only a small portion of the left and right sides of your brain. In this space, you find a direct access to your senses, pure and undiluted. Remain in this center and observe the shift in consciousness.

You are accessing a simple and pure level of consciousness that can be described as animalistic. This is only one of many levels of consciousness that humans use to create their experience of reality. It is beneficial to occasionally isolate this level of awareness and allow it to dominate while in a meditative space.

This aspect of consciousness is a vital and necessary part of who you are. Honor and celebrate it. Visualize yourself as an animal with simple needs and desires. Allow the more complex aspects of your consciousness to fall away. Use your senses without expectations or ulterior motives. Allow yourself to experience the moment by unconditionally observing your sensory input.

To fully recognize the presence and potential of Ok, you must release ideas of who you are and allow your sensory input to create your experience of the moment. This is an unconditional and surrendered way of being. It is the essence of trust and the ability to accept without judgment. It is important to allow this trusting and accepting aspect of consciousness to motivate your actions on occasion. By doing this, you reopen to Ok's gift of consciousness and reconnect with its presence.

To work more consciously with Ok, it is necessary to be in the moment and allow yourself to be in a trusting and open state. By allowing the animal consciousness within to survive and exist without threatening it with complex attitudes and ideas, you create a balance necessary for a healthy existence.

NOTES AND INSIGHTS:

CHUEN

TRADITIONAL: Monkey
DREAMSPELL: Blue Monkey
KICHÉ: Batz'

ICON: The round form near the top of the icon represents the coming together of two different levels of consciousness as one. This also depicts their equal influence. The two forms on either side represent the two states of consciousness that the monkey carries. The bottom configuration represents the reproductive nature of the interplay between these two polarized, male and female, states of consciousness.

ESSENCE: Chuen is essentially the creativity of union and the enjoyment of the creative process.

SYMBOL: Chuen is symbolized by a monkey, because they are creative and delight in the process of life. Monkeys maintain a balance between a primal and a more evolved awareness.

MANIFESTATIONS: Those who are experiencing Chuen's presence may feel an energetic high and a positive sense of power in their ability to responsibly create their reality.

On Chuen's day, you may experience creative, artistic desires and abilities, an openness to play and an ability to enjoy life. It's a day to be a conscious co-creator and a joyful, positive participant in the creation of life.

Those born with Chuen as their Daykeeper may be happy-go-lucky, enjoy responsibility or be envied by others for their good fortune.

KEY WORDS: art, celebration, craftsman, delight, enjoyment, happy, interplay, laughing, lucky, magic, monkey, play, pleasure, sex and union.

Chuen brings together two levels of consciousness. These include a basic level that can be recognized as sensual and animalistic as well as a more evolved perception of the consequences of actions and the ability to perceive or expect future outcomes. There is a balanced union between these two levels of consciousness that stimulates play and enjoyment in what could be considered a naive, yet aware way.

MEDITATION FOR CHUEN

Relax and focus on the image of Chuen, either on the icon before you or in your mind. Breathe yourself into a more relaxed state. Allow your consciousness to focus near the center of your brain, including a large portion of the left and right halves of your brain. Observe the shift in consciousness as you remain centered in this area.

It is here that you access a primal and pure sensual awareness, as well as the ability to perceive possible future outcomes. What is noticeably absent from this center is fear. This trusting and open level of consciousness is always accessible to you. By remaining focused on this level, you allow the more complex and stressful effects of fear and anxiety to dissipate.

Envision the monkey and its simple and joyful way of relating to its environment. It observes without judgment. It is accepting, yet its cautiousness comes from a true perception rather than an irrational fear. Chuen delights in its surroundings with unconditional ease. It is beneficial for you to access this simpler level of consciousness. As it strengthens your less complex mind, it balances your perception of reality as a whole.

To work consciously with Chuen, it is necessary to release fear. Simply allow your perception of possible outcomes to guide you to your truest desire. It is necessary to be present in the moment with an open and unconditional perception of the possible future. Allow wonderment and delight to guide you. Chuen can lead you to a more relaxed way of relating to your environment.

When we as humans are willing to give up the complexities that fear and judgment create, we will then allow ourselves to become more of what we already are: a simple, natural and evolved race of beings.

NOTES AND INSIGHTS:

EB

TRADITIONAL: Grass or Tooth
DREAMSPELL: Yellow Human
KICHÉ: E

ICON: The form to the upper right on the icon represents an open mind. This acts as an open vessel for a higher consciousness to enter into. The dots coming off this form represent the movement of a higher awareness permeating the rest of human consciousness. The face represents the human form.

ESSENCE: Eb is essentially a guide from beyond. Eb is a guardian being who comes into time and space and maintains an awareness of what lies beyond time and space.

SYMBOL: The tooth carries within it the potential of the human being. This can be recognized as destiny. It is what will become of the human race as a result of its relationship with its past and its ancestors. The tooth represents both the ancestry and future of humanity.

MANIFESTATIONS: Eb often appears as a guide or a powerful force that assists you on your journey. Eb may come to you from within or through someone else.

On days with Eb as Daykeeper, you may more easily access spiritual awareness and expanded states of consciousness. It is a good day to contact inner guides or draw inspiration to attain a higher perspective on daily affairs.

Those born with Eb as their Daykeeper have a natural ability to attain a spiritual, expanded awareness. When inspired, they can guide others to their true path to begin fulfilling their higher purpose.

KEY WORDS: channeling, destiny, guide, higher mind, human being, inspiration, path, spiritual, tooth and wisdom.

Eb acts as a channel that connects our human consciousness with our spiritual or higher mind. This includes the act of receiving answers or information from a source that appears to dwell beyond our conscious minds. It is our link to an all-knowing aspect of consciousness.

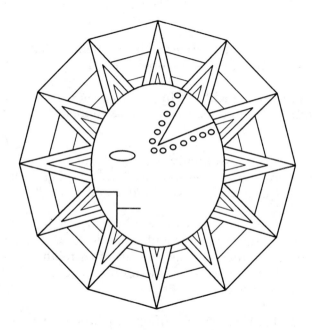

MEDITATION FOR EB

Relax and focus on the image of Eb, either on the icon before you or in your mind. Breathe yourself into a more relaxed state. Focus on the center at the top of your skull. This is the open, soft area on the top of a newborn baby's head that closes as the baby grows. Envision a cord that connects your consciousness at this place with a more infinite, all-knowing aspect of yourself, or what could be considered the higher mind.

Observe where the cord touches the boundary of your physical body. Notice whether this cord appears sealed shut or open. Allow it to open completely so that your connection to your higher mind is accessible to your conscious mind. Relax and keep your focus on this opening. Release any expectations and be here now.

You may want to access new information by asking questions while in this open state. Allow the answers to come through, seeping into your consciousness and filling who you know yourself to be with a higher truth.

The more you practice meditation with Eb, the easier it becomes to recognize Eb's ability to channel information into your conscious mind. This occurs almost continually throughout our daily lives. When we are unaware of Eb's inspiration, the information gets filtered through our conscious minds and is often distorted. To work more consciously with Eb, focus on the precise moment of receiving information or answers from a higher source so that it can be received in its purest form, undiluted and unchanged by your conscious awareness. This can be done by consciously seeking answers or other information from the higher mind.

Nearly all the inspiration and revelations we receive travels through this channel from a collective consciousness, or what could be perceived as our higher minds. This is a place in consciousness where everything is one. Eb can be a guide to our own immortality by connecting with an ever-living, never-ending source of consciousness. We must remember that we are ultimately all one, and that all ideas originate from the same source.

NOTES AND INSIGHTS:

BEN

TRADITIONAL: Cane or Reed
DREAMSPELL: Red Skywalker
KICHÉ: Aj

ICON: The two forms near the top of the icon represent nourishment for growth, such as water coming down to nourish a plant. The two forms on the bottom of the icon represent the interconnection of growth and family. The horizontal line connects the growth, similar to how certain grasses or cane are intertwined or connected.

ESSENCE: Ben is the awareness of the family and the family line. It is a connection to ancestors as well as future generations. Ben is also the oneness and joy that can be discovered within a unified family.

SYMBOL: The cane plant represents the intricate and dependent relationships within a large family. It symbolizes the difficulty of surviving alone without support.

MANIFESTATIONS: Ben expresses in the human experience as the awareness of family, including both ancestors and the future potential of the family.

On a Ben day, there may be a general focus on the family or other dependent relationships. You may feel more intimate with others around you. Be careful not to engage those close to you in obsolete family patterns.

Those born with Ben as their Daykeeper are often responsible and devoted family members. They may assume the responsibility of being the caretaker of the family.

KEY WORDS: cane, clan, dependent, devotion, family, folk, holding hands, household, kin, kindred, intimate, offspring, reed, relations, responsible and supportive.

Ben brings together the interconnectedness of the family and the nourishment that supports the family. This creates a supportive environment for the family to live in. There is a quality of nourishment that brings a family together. What is nourishing for some is destructive for others. Each individual seeks out what feeds him or her and sustains the life within. The coming together of individuals to seek out and receive what nourishes and sustains their lives is the essence of family. It is each individual's responsibility to find the most supportive place to live or plant oneself, so to speak. In doing this, you may find yourself attached to and related to others who have sought out the same source of nourishment.

There are many levels to the experience of family. There is the basic fundamental level of direct kinship, and the level at which an entire species can be recognized as a family. The family experience can grow to include all life. There is also a more spiritual experience of family that happens when a group seeks out a similar quality from what appears to be a spiritual source.

MEDITATION FOR BEN

Focus on the image of Ben, either on the icon before you or in your mind. Relax and breathe yourself into a more relaxed state. Visualize yourself as a plant that has roots growing into the ground. You receive nourishment through these roots as well as from the Sun and the rain that come from above. Observe yourself growing. You are reaching outward and becoming a vine. Some parts of the vine take root into the Earth, a direct source of nourishment. Some are dependent on their nourishment coming to them through the plant itself. Each leaf, flower or fruit of the vine may appear to be singular, but in reality it is one plant connected to one source. This is the essence of family. If one part of the plant becomes damaged or weakened, it affects the entire plant.

Much in the same way that each part of the plant is connected to and affected by the rest of the plant, you as an individual are connected to and affected by your family, humanity and all of life. It is important to recognize that the source and nourishment for all life is ultimately love.

To work more consciously with Ben, you must visualize yourself as a part of something vast and eternal. You must recognize yourself within everything you see. By negating or judging something that appears to be outside you, you are only cutting yourself off from a source of love and support. It is important to release all judgments and accept yourself as an emanation of love, as a creation of love and as a child of love.

NOTES AND INSIGHTS:

IX

TRADITIONAL: Jaguar
DREAMSPELL: White Wizard
KICHÉ: Ish

ICON: The circular form at the top of the icon represents individual consciousness. The three large dots or features portray the face of the jaguar. The spots represent an opening through which spirit freely moves in and out.

ESSENCE: Ix's essence is the spirit world's interrelationship with the physical dimensions of the Earth.

SYMBOL: The jaguar represents both powerful spirit and powerful Earth. It symbolizes a balanced relationship between the two. The jaguar is open to the influence of spirit. It represents an openness to the influence and movement of spirit throughout its entire body. The jaguar is capable of living and being seen in the physical world as well as the spiritual world. Its spirit body, when traveling in other dimensions, also appears as a jaguar.

MANIFESTATIONS: Ix may manifest as an awareness of spirit and what may be considered supernatural.

On an Ix day, you may want to be more open to messages from the spirit world. It is a good day to contemplate who you are in dimensions of life other than just the material and physical.

Those born on an Ix day have the ability to perceive the spirit within. They can respond to this spirit and receive its communication while in the physical world.

KEY WORDS: disappear, Earth spirit, freedom, interdimensional, jaguar, reappear, receptivity, spirit, spots, supernatural and withdraw.

Ix represents a spiritual and material consciousness. Ix manifests on a level where a spiritual existence can maintain an individual consciousness. Ix works through and with the physical form as well as other dimensions of existence.

MEDITATION FOR IX

Relax and focus on the image of Ix, either on the icon before you or in your mind. Breathe yourself into a more relaxed state. Visualize the jaguar. Observe the jaguar in your mind walking through the jungle. It has the ability to seemingly disappear and reappear at will. A quality that is vital to the jaguar's existence is its ability to disengage from its individual consciousness and form, to blend with its surroundings. It uses its will as an individual to become nonexistent as an individual.

Return your consciousness back to your body. Allow your consciousness to expand to include your surroundings. Fill the immediate surroundings with your consciousness. Become your surroundings and allow your physical form to melt into it, lose your individuality and become part of the scenery. Not only is this skill important while hunting, it is most important to disengage from the illusions of self-identity. Many ideas of who we are come from how others see us. To become nonexistent for a moment in time is to release false ideas of who we are. It is a way to reconnect with our spiritual identity that lives beyond physical forms.

Ix represents a unique spiritual level where the spirit has an individual consciousness and will, yet does not completely attach itself to a material form. This is a level where a spirit has a conscious choice of what form it will take and whether or not it will take form. This level of awareness is only accessible by a direct and specific path. This is an advanced state of consciousness. It involves remembering and recognizing your life purpose beyond the illusory self created by your ego or your sense of identity.

To work more consciously with Ix, you must recognize the benefit and potential of releasing the identity based on your physical form and material surroundings. It is necessary to detach from your physical form and acknowledge a spiritual level of self that existed before this body was created and will continue to exist after it is gone. The benefit of maintaining this level of awareness is to access a higher purpose for the individual form you have chosen. Ix is a guide to the ability to use and manifest form in the most effective and appropriate way that allows spirit to work through it.

NOTES AND INSIGHTS:

MEN

TRADITIONAL: Bird or Eagle
DREAMSPELL: Blue Eagle
KICHÉ: Tzikin

ICON: The space on the top of the icon represents a clear and open mind. The dots coming off the eye represent inner vision, the ability to look within the mind. The vertical lines near the bottom represent feathers. The face is that of a bird or a human.

ESSENCE: Men is essentially mental clarity and focus, with the ability to envision and create abundance.

SYMBOL: The bird represents and carries the ability to mentally focus and envision possibilities greater than itself. It has the ability to see things from a distance and use its expanded perspective to see more of the bigger picture.

MANIFESTATIONS: Men often manifests as a new idea or vision. With this comes the ability to recognize a new goal or desire and opportunities not apparent to others. Men may visit you with a clear vision of your potential for wealth and well-being.

On Men's day, you can benefit from visualizing your true desires. Be open to new ideas and unexpected insights. Take the steps required to enhance your wealth and well-being.

Those born with Men as their Daykeeper are natural producers and visionaries. They can envision and bring together the resources needed for the manifestation of something larger than themselves, something that involves the work and input of many people.

KEY WORDS: abundance, achieve, bird, clarity, coins, envision, fly, focus, insight, mind, money, produce, prosper, visionary, wealth and well-being.

Men is the ability to look within and have a direct and clear focus on any given situation. Men brings together the analytical and decisive mind. To have a complete understanding of a situation, you must cut away distractions and focus directly on solutions or the ultimate goal. It is the ability to expand beyond your own direct relationship with any given situation or event and see the larger, more complete picture to recognize the relatedness of all things.

MEDITATION FOR MEN

Relax and focus on the image of Men, either on the icon before you or in your mind. Breathe yourself into a more relaxed state. Visualize yourself as a bird. You are a bird of prey sitting on top of a high tree, looking down on to the landscape. You have the ability to observe the interrelations of all things around you. You recognize movement and see what it is, based on its position in the environment. You have a direct knowing of how to achieve your goals. You know exactly what you want and how to get it.

It is beneficial for you to access this level of consciousness in times when you feel there is a solution needed or goal to be clarified. Men is a guide that will assist you in directly accessing your inner mental clarity. This state of consciousness will guide you out of confusion. It will lead you up, to a clear place to view what is necessary to achieve and manifest your true desires.

Find an unclear or confusing situation in your mind. Visualize Men as a bird that comes to take these confusing thoughts and leads your consciousness to a higher viewpoint. Allow Men to guide you and reveal what is true, what is needed for achieving your goal and what is no longer necessary or beneficial.

To work more consciously with Men, you must be willing to perceive yourself and your surroundings with a clear and focused vision. You must be willing to release confusion and doubt. The more you utilize this level of consciousness, the more focused your mind will become. Men is a mental state where all answers come directly into your consciousness without the need to ask questions. You must be willing to give up all preconceived ideas of who you are and what you want.

Allow all expectations to dissolve. It is necessary to stay present in the moment and trust your inner vision. When this inner vision is awakened and utilized, the ability to manifest your true desires will become strong. It is important to refrain from manipulating or trying to control what you believe are your desires. It takes commitment and honesty to become aware of what you truly desire and to release false expectations.

NOTES AND INSIGHTS:

KIB

TRADITIONAL: *Vulture, Owl or Spider*
DREAMSPELL: *Yellow Warrior*
KICHÉ: *Ajmak'*

ICON: The spiraling form in the center of the icon represents disconnected consciousness or a solitary figure in a solitary space. The circle around this figure creates the disconnection or the solitary space. The lines connecting to this circle represent the influence from beyond the solitude.

ESSENCE: The essence of Kib is the experience of solitude.

SYMBOL: The vulture separates itself from other living things by preying on the dead. It feeds off of completion, rather than interacting with others and maintaining ongoing relationships.

MANIFESTATIONS: You may experience Kib as the need for solitude or the desire for separation. Being alone is often necessary to unwind from intimate or entangled interactions with others. Kib's gifts are given to those who can be alone with themselves.

On a day with Kib as Daykeeper, you may want to find time to be by yourself or focus on what you can do by yourself alone. It's an opportune time to separate yourself from those people and things that no longer serve your current needs. You may feel much better after bringing certain things to a final completion.

People born on a Kib day often experience their most profound revelations in solitude and usually work best alone. Even in the presence of others they are able to maintain an independent awareness of self.

KEY WORDS: alone, detached, disconnected, divorce, independent, isolated, lone, owl, privacy, remote, retirement, selfish, separate, single, solitary, solo, spider and vulture.

Kib creates solitude for a more in-depth experience of the singular self. Kib is like a baby in the womb. It lives in solitary space, yet it is nurtured or influenced by something that seems to be outside of the space. It is necessary to be alone for certain growth processes to take place. To accurately form a sense of identity, you must detach from your environment and release the influences imposed by others.

MEDITATION FOR KIB

Focus on the image of Kib, either on the icon before you or in your mind. Breathe yourself into a more relaxed state. Imagine yourself as a baby inside a womb. The space around you is soft, dark and fluid. Everything you see is within the womb that surrounds you. Relax into this space and allow your consciousness to stay focused in the womb. It is in this apparently isolated space that you receive the nurturing necessary for you to become who you are. Expand your consciousness and realize that you are within the womb of a mother. You can hear her heartbeat and her voice. You feel her joy or sorrow.

Kib incorporates the solitary experience with the awareness that there is more than yourself. You are connected to the world around you. To maintain a sense of identity is to understand your relationship to your world. The understanding of this relationship can grow and evolve when you allow yourself to reflect within your inner solitary space. At times it is necessary to create detachment so that you may redefine your experience of yourself and the world around you. You may then reconnect yourself in a more appropriate and beneficial way.

To work with Kib more consciously, you must be willing to detach yourself from what appear to be outside influences. The more difficult you find this to be, the more necessary it is. It is important to recognize that remaining attached to outside influences that do not support or promote your growth as an individual, is not only sabotaging your own growth process, but also the growth process of those who are influencing you. It is necessary to look at your relationship with your world without judgment. Simply observe whether you are receiving the support you need. If you are not receiving the necessary support, it is likely that you are not caring for and giving support to your environment and others around you. To whatever degree there is a lack of support, it is necessary to reevaluate your relationships with other individuals as well as with your environment. It is a natural growth process within the structure of life to separate in order to grow. It is love that motivates growth and evolution. Allow love to guide you during this process.

NOTES AND INSIGHTS:

KABAN

TRADITIONAL: *Incense, Movement or Quake*
DREAMSPELL: *Red Earth*
KICHÉ: *Noj*

ICON: The form to the left on the icon represents a fluid, open mind with free-flowing thoughts. The ascending circles portray upward movement to a higher level of thought. The line above connects and shows the balance between these two states of consciousness. It also represents how both are equally necessary to access Kaban's potential.

ESSENCE: Kaban is essentially the abilities of the human mind. This includes programming thought, the potential positive and negative effects of thought, and the evolution of the human mind.

SYMBOL: Burning incense represents the possible reaches and effects of mental activities.

MANIFESTATIONS: Kaban may be experienced as mental cleansing, possibly mental clarity and, often, mental over-whelm.

On a Kaban day, you may clear your mind by watching the movement and content of your thinking without attachment or judgment. This will enable you to think more clearly and focus your thoughts on a higher level of consciousness.

Those born with Kaban as their Daykeeper tend to have unique mental abilities with a potential to be clear thinkers. These talents can be used to access higher levels of consciousness and effectively resolve conflicts and complex problems.

KEY WORDS: clarity, conclude, confusion, evolve, genius, headache, incense, innovative, intelligence, meditation, mind, movement, navigate, patience, resolve, think and thought.

Kaban is the highest potential of the mind. The more fluid and open your thought processes, the more potential there is of evolving to a new level of conceptualizing. Kaban awakens and encourages new growth out of old ways of thinking. Kaban works with individual minds as well as with collective consciousness.

MEDITATION FOR KABAN

Relax and focus on the image of Kaban, either on the icon before you or in your mind. Breathe yourself into a more relaxed state. Relax your mind and allow your thoughts to flow freely. Watch your thoughts as if you were watching a movie. Relax and open your mind by detaching from all thoughts. When you detach from them, allowing them to exist without attempting to control or manipulate them, you allow for a natural evolution in your thought process.

Envision your thoughts or ideas enclosed within bubbles that are floating away from you. The bubbles pop and the thoughts are gone. By relaxing and opening your mind, you are releasing all unnecessary thought patterns. By releasing the patterns that no longer serve you, you have access to a more evolved way of thinking.

Your thought process creates your experience of reality. It is necessary to clear your mind so that your reality is in tune with the present moment. Unnecessary thought patterns can entrap you and keep you from experiencing the moment. This is a mental karma that must be consciously released in order to free it and your consciousness. Many unnecessary thought patterns re-create an experience that was somehow traumatic to you. Sometimes these thought patterns are passed from one generation to the next. This re-creates an experience passed on from your mother or father or even from those who preceded them.

To work consciously with Kaban, it is important to go into a relaxed and meditative state. Releasing unnecessary thought patterns is a natural process. The more relaxed and open you become, the more your thoughts evolve and become attuned with the present moment. It is important to trust the process and not attempt to control it in any way. Continue to relax and open your mind. By doing this, you allow a new reality and a new way of relating to the world and yourself to unfold before you. This is an invitation to release the trauma that holds you in an imbalanced relationship with yourself and the world. It is an invitation to participate in the present moment and allow your relationship with yourself and the world to be in balance and harmony.

NOTES AND INSIGHTS:

ETZ'NAB

TRADITIONAL: Flint Knife
DREAMSPELL: White Mirror
KICHÉ: Tijash

ICON: This image symbolizes a crack or sharp cuts, a shattering of the whole and a transformation.

ESSENCE: Etz'nab is the essence of sacrifice. It is giving up the positive aspects of life for the moment. Etz'nab brings change and sometimes destruction in order to achieve transformation.

SYMBOL: The knife symbolizes cutting away from the source of sickness or creating a separation that allows new growth.

MANIFESTATIONS: When present, Etz'nab may stimulate a powerful awakening to anger and the need for change. It can appear as rage or the destruction of an old form. Through sudden events or changes, Etz'nab may provoke you to be more present in the moment.

Etz'nab days provide an opportunity to detach from obsolete motivations and future expectations. You may want to voluntarily arrive in the present moment. Recognize that when something or someone outside you appears to interrupt you by demanding your attention, you are being invited into the moment.

Those born with Etz'nab as their Daykeeper are people who recognize and express the need for change. Their actions often challenge the status quo and can create change for themselves and others.

KEY WORDS: anger, break, broken mirror, crack, cut, destruction, dispute, divide, fight, knife, rage, sacrifice, sharp, shatter, split, suffering, transformation and war.

Etz'nab is the cracked outer shell that allows access into a deeper level. Etz'nab responds to outer influences by enforcing transformation. To fully understand this process, you must recognize the inner workings of whole systems in relationship to the whole. There is an infinite relationship connecting all things and a chain reaction of constant transformation that affects all things.

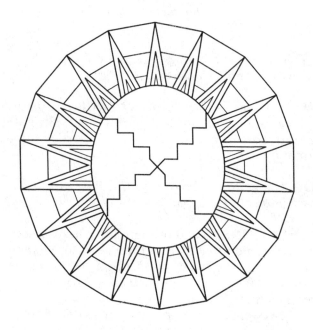

MEDITATION FOR ETZ'NAB

Focus on the image of Etz'nab, either on the icon before you or in your mind. Breathe yourself into a more relaxed state. Visualize the Earth. Deep inside the Earth are the tectonic plates. Their movement in relationship to each other creates a pressure that shakes and cracks the Earth's surface. The subsequent earthquake that occurs is the essence of Etz'nab's transformational qualities.

Allow your consciousness to focus on the part of your life that is experiencing pressure at this time. This can be a physical experience as well as a feeling or mental experience. Recognize this pressure as the first stage of a transformation occurring in your life. You are responding to outer or inner changes that travel through you and continue onward. Welcome the transformation and trust that it will create a balance between you and the inner or outer pressure.

Etz'nab is not transformation by growth, it is transformation by destruction. The destruction breaks away what is no longer appropriate or in harmony with its surroundings. An inner experience with Etz'nab is anger. It is not always appropriate to identify with the anger and allow it to motivate your actions. The anger is the pressure that creates the transformation. If you hold onto the anger, it can block the creative flow and inhibit the transformation from occurring as a natural process. It is important to recognize that anger, especially when directed at something or someone, should be released and transformed with ease. It is not a natural state for anyone to maintain the experience of anger for more than a brief moment.

To work consciously with Etz'nab, you must be willing to trust the transformational process and allow all anger to be released and completed. It is important to recognize that holding onto anger will only perpetuate tension and irritation and inhibit the possibility of change. When anger is released, transformation is able to flow naturally and create balance. You must practice releasing anger in relationship to everything and everyone. When this done, the experience of transformation becomes more harmonious and balanced.

NOTES AND INSIGHTS:

KAWAK

TRADITIONAL: Rain or Storm
DREAMSPELL: Blue Storm
KICHÉ: Kawok'

ICON: The circles near the top of the icon represent a cloud. The jagged line coming down from the cloud represents lightning. The "X" marks where the lightning strikes or makes contact. The form to the left, near the bottom, represents the resulting transformation. This can be either a splitting of one into two or a never-ending, spiraling evolution. The marks surrounding this form represent the energetic environment or aura of what is being transformed.

ESSENCE: Kawak's essence is sudden transformation. It is instantaneous creation and revelation. It is a change that often takes place without recognition because of its swiftness.

SYMBOL: The storm cloud represents sudden change. Where do the lightning and thunder manifest from? Each appears to come from itself alone. It is this unknown force within the cloud that represents Kawak.

MANIFESTATIONS: You may experience Kawak as an immediate shift in consciousness, a powerful force or a loud, violent noise.

On a day with Kawak as Daykeeper, you are invited to acknowledge and respect life's mysteries and all that is beyond your power to control.

Those born on a Kawak day feel a part of something that is beyond normal human consciousness. Their deepest motivations often remain a mystery even to themselves.

KEY WORDS: catalyst, cloud, electric, enigma, explosive, instantaneous, fire, lightning, loud, mystery, originate, shift, storm, sudden, thunder and unexpected.

Kawak is complete and sudden transformation. It is an abrupt ending that thoroughly completes, then suddenly begins something new. Kawak is mysterious and practical. It is a level of existence where there is no physical matter, only energy. The laws of physical nature do not apply at this level of being.

MEDITATION FOR KAWAK

Focus on the image of Kawak, either on the icon before you or in your mind. Breathe yourself into a more relaxed state. Envision a storm cloud traveling toward you. It is full of energy and life. It is dark and thick, rumbling as it travels. Envision lightning traveling between the Earth's surface and the cloud. The cloud has an energetic relationship with the land. The Earth receives energy from the cloud and also sends energy into it through the lightning bolts. The storm has a balancing effect on the Earth, because it allows for the release of energy buildups as well as increases the levels of energy where it has been depleted.

Recognize yourself as an energy being. You are created from energy that exists at several different frequencies. These range from the highest, almost unrecognizable frequency, to the densest one that creates your physical body. All energy can be transformed into a higher frequency if the proper connection is made. It is Kawak who makes the connection that transforms energy, much like a lightning bolt.

To realize the energetic potential of all things is to come closer to accessing Kawak's practical level of being. It is Kawak's mysterious nature that is unpredictable and cannot be easily understood. To work consciously with Kawak, you must surrender to the unknown and accept the possibility that there is an inherent organization within the apparent chaos. An experience of Kawak may include an unmistakable life-changing event. It is a shift that is so sudden and transformative that it is difficult or impossible to identify with your past or what previously motivated you. Kawak transforms on the most fundamental level. This level is usually unrecognizable, so the transformation comes without conscious warning.

Kawak can awaken you to a more organized and systematic universe. As unpredictable as it may appear from a familiar level of consciousness, the more you become aware of the fundamental and energetic level of all things, the more you can recognize the sacred order of life. As individuals and humanity become more conscious of these inner workings, we will recognize more clearly the sacredness of all things.

NOTES AND INSIGHTS:

AHAW

TRADITIONAL: *Flower, Hunter or Lord*
DREAMSPELL: *Yellow Sun*
KICHÉ: *Ajpú*

ICON: The two circles near the center of the icon represent seeing with open eyes. The round form near the bottom represents speaking with an open mouth. The vertical lines represent a direct connection between consciousness and communication. The whole face represents an open and evolved being.

ESSENCE: The essence of Ahaw is the completion, the encompassing and the understanding of the journey.

SYMBOL: Ahaw is symbolized by a human face. On this face is written both the life of the individual and the lives of his or her ancestors. The face reveals the effects of the passage of time through successive generations.

MANIFESTATIONS: Ahaw may be experienced as a sense of completion. This experience may include understanding the causes and effects that led to this moment. Ahaw offers the awareness of how completion relates to the entire cycle of life.

Ahaw's days are opportunities to see situations as they fit into the bigger picture. It is a good time to consider the necessity of certain events and their involvement in something larger than their immediate effects.

People born on an Ahaw day are sensitive to the cycles of time and respect the importance of being timely. They naturally accept that everything plays a part in something greater than itself.

KEY WORDS: all-seeing, complete, comprehensive, conscientious, cyclic, encompass, end, fruition, omniscient, punctual, regular, time and timely.

Ahaw is the completion of a journey and the wisdom that is gained from the journey. It is a deep understanding of the purpose of events. Ahaw's presence signifies an ending of something significant, only with the full realization of its significance in the moment.

MEDITATION FOR AHAW

Focus on the image of Ahaw, either on the icon before you or in your mind. Relax and breathe yourself into a more relaxed state. Observe the open, receptive face that creates Ahaw's image. It is in the face that we recognize the sincerity of an individual. We can recognize the life they have lived as well as the lives of their ancestors. The journeys that have been taken and completed are revealed in the face.

Observe your face in a mirror or in your mind. Recognize that in this moment a completion is occurring; a realization is being made. Look at who you are. Observe how much of your experience of who you are is based on where you have been and what you have done up until this moment. In this moment are you here, present with what is being completed? In this moment are you remembering the past, or do you have expectations for the future? It is important to answer these questions honestly without judgment. Do you understand why you are here in this place at this time?

It is important to take responsibility for where you are now and accept the path that you have taken and the journey you are on is sacred and profound. To work consciously with Ahaw, it is necessary to allow yourself the experience of understanding. Complete the past and hold no expectations for the future. In order to complete, you must be present on your path and make a conscious choice to be with yourself where you are.

Ahaw is an awakener into time. It is the realization of time and the effects of time. It is the ability to find this moment in time and observe its relationship to a larger cycle. Your experience of time reveals your relationship with it. Your experience and concept of time transforms and changes as you evolve toward a more present, centered state of consciousness. It is important to welcome the experience of time and receive it as a gift. It is perfect as it is in this moment. There is no need to run from it, race though it or attempt to slow it down. These attempts reveal how distant you are from the moment. Ahaw is a true presence in the moment and an unconditional acceptance that transcends time and allows for the experience of eternity.

NOTES AND INSIGHTS:

INTRODUCING THE MAYA CALENDAR

What is commonly called the Maya calendar is composed of a number of cycles of varying lengths and purposes. The more familiar components of the Maya calendar are the 260-day Tzol'Kin cycle, the 365-day Haab cycle and an over 5000-year cycle called the Long Count. These three cycles and many others are all interconnected, interdependent and integral aspects of what we call the Maya calendar.

Time is based on movement. The movement of the Earth as it spins around and rotates along its axis is measured in days. The Earth revolves around the Sun, and this movement is counted in years. Calendars are tools to keep track of two or more cycles of time. Recognizing and honoring the archetypal energies that are present in time is a way of making time sacred. Astrology is the awareness of the archetypal presence that exists within different periods of time.

The Maya perception of time differs from the common view in three significant ways. The Maya view recognizes that time is cyclic and only appears to be linear. It is also significant when two or more cycles begin or end at the same time. A third ingredient of the Maya conception of time is the awareness of the archetypal or spiritual presence within each portion of time. Each day and cycle has its deity or guiding spirit.

TZOL'KIN

Many of the cycles recognized by the ancient Maya have also been acknowledged and used by other cultures. One cycle and calendar used by the Maya and other indigenous peoples of Mexico and Central America is unique and extraordinary. One of the Maya names for this 260-day cycle and calendar is

Tzol'Kin. The Tzol'Kin day-count and cycle is considered to be the most sacred aspect of the entire Maya calendar. Within the Tzol'Kin cycle, the archetypal or spiritual presence of each day is called a Daykeeper. There are twenty Daykeepers represented by twenty day-signs. The movement of these twenty Daykeepers creates a twenty-day cycle. This twenty-day cycle is not based on any movement of the Earth or any movement of the planets within our solar system. The twenty Daykeepers are an expression of a movement within our Galaxy. Built around the Tzol'Kin are cycles of the Sun, the Earth, the Moon and other planets in our solar system. All these cycles are synchronized to the galactic tone as carried by the movement of the Daykeepers.

Each day of the Tzol'Kin count is identified by a number from one to thirteen and by one of twenty archetypal Daykeepers or day-signs. Thirteen numbers matched with twenty Daykeepers offers 260 possible combinations. Each day is followed through the entire 260-day sequence as a calendar made up of thirteen-day cycles and twenty-day cycles. This is repeated perpetually. The devotion to maintaining this continuous tradition and sacred counting of days is still practiced today among contemporary Maya. In Maya astrology, your birth sign and Daykeeper come from the day of the Tzol'Kin you were born on.

Currently, there are two different Tzol'Kin counts that are in popular use. One is the traditional count that has remained unchanged and consistent for all the indigenous people of Mesoamerica for thousands of years. The count followed by human daykeepers in Guatemala today can be traced through the Aztec period back to the ancient Maya culture. While the names and attributes may have been different, the day-count has remained unchanged and consistent, suggesting an unbroken tradition and transmission. There is no other cycle in the Maya calendar or no other calendar from Mesoamerica that is so honored.

Since the time of Harmonic Convergence, August 16-17, 1987, there has been a renewed interest in the Maya calendar and the Tzol'Kin. The 1987 publication of the book, *The Mayan Factor*, and the release of the *Dreamspell Game* in 1992 have assisted many non-Maya to recognize and work with the Tzol'Kin. The Tzol'Kin count popularized through these works is referred to in this book as the New Age Tzol'Kin. It is different from the "Traditional" Tzol'Kin in three significant ways.

The day-signs derived from the New Age Tzol'Kin are different from those obtained from the Traditional system. While both are 260-day long cycles with the same internal consistency, the dates for each are different. For example, December 21, 2012, according to the New Age Tzol'Kin, is a "12-Manik" day. According to the Traditional Tzol'Kin, it is a "4-Ahaw" day.

Those who learned about the Tzol'Kin through the *Dreamspell Game* or its offshoot, the *Thirteen-Moon Calendar*, also use a different terminology for the day names. "12-Manik" is referred to as "Blue Crystal Hand" in "Dreamspeak," the lingo spoken by followers of *Dreamspell*. This is the second significant difference.

The third significant difference between these two Tzol'Kin counts is that the New Age Tzol'Kin skips February 29 every four years, but the Traditional Tzol'Kin counts it as a day. This indicates that every four years the Traditional Tzol'Kin advances one day faster than the New Age Tzol'Kin. After February 29, 1996, the two Tzol'Kin counts were 51 days apart, then 50 days after February 29, 2000. This phasing continues until February 29, 2208, when the two counts become synchronized and essentially the same during the next four years, through February 28, 2212.

HAAB

A 365-day cycle that makes up a part of the Maya calendar is called Haab. It is usually counted as eighteen months of twenty days each, with a nineteenth month of five days added at the end. A 365-day cycle was also used by the ancient Egyptians; 365 days is nearly the time it takes for the Earth to orbit the Sun. We call the period of this orbit a year and modern astronomy calculates it to be 365.2419 days. This indicates that our year is almost a quarter of a day, or about 6 hours longer, than the 365-day Haab cycle.

Many cultures and religions use different days to begin their yearly calendar or celebrate the New Year. There are also a number of different starting dates for the Haab cycle. There are Haab cycles that begin in January, February, March, July and December, to mention only a few. Since the introduction of the European-style Julian and Gregorian calendars into Mesoamerica, there are presently two distinct types of Haab.

One type of Haab basically ignores the Julian and Gregorian calendars. Since these Haab calendars do not take Leap Day into consideration, their starting dates shift one day earlier every four years when compared with the modern calendar. For example, February 26, 1996, was New Year's Day for Kiché Maya in Guatemala. Since 1996 was a leap year, their New Year's Day in 1997 was February 25. It will be February 25 every year until the year 2001, when it arrives on February 24, according to the modern calendar.

The other type of yearly Haab calendars are called "frozen" calendars because they start their new year on the same day every year according to either the Julian or Gregorian calendar. Examples of this are the Aztec calendar, which begins its new year on January 17 (Julian), since it "froze" in 1610; and the Tzotzil calendar which starts December 28 (Gregorian), since it "froze" in 1688. A traditional Maya Haab calendar from Mayapan "froze" its starting date to July 16 (Julian) in the year 1553 and hence, July 26 (Gregorian). At least a dozen "frozen" calendars have been documented in Mesoamerica with different starting dates for the new year. All these "frozen" calendars skip Leap Day.

Counting 260-day Tzol'Kin cycles and 365-day Haab cycles, starting on the same day, brings these two cycles back together in about 52 years. After seventy-three (73 x 260) Tzol'Kin have cycled and fifty-two (52 x 365) Haab have cycled, these two counts end on the same day and start together again on the next day. Seventy-three Tzol'Kin are composed of 18,980 days, the same number of days in fifty-two 365-day Haab cycles. Since there are a variety of different starting dates for the Haab, there are a number of different 52-year cycles considered in the Maya calendar. This kind of interweaving of cycles is an integral part of the Maya calendar.

Another example of this coming together of cycles includes starting a 584-day Venus cycle on the same day as a Tzol'Kin and a Haab, bringing these three cycles together in about 104 years. In 37,960 days, exactly 104 Haab have cycled, exactly 146 Tzol'Kin have also cycled and 65 Venus cycles have come to pass.

The Tzol'Kin can be seen as a way of receiving messages from the Galaxy. In a similar way, yearly calendars and Haab calendars carry messages from the Sun. Each different yearly calendar may be recognized as carrying different information or frequencies from and through the Sun. The calendars that start July 26 may carry messages from the star Sirius through the Sun to the Earth, since this is the day that Sirius heliacally rises at dawn in the northern Yucatan, near sacred sites such as Mayapan and Chichén Itzá. A yearly calendar that starts in December would carry frequencies from the stars of Ophiuchus, since the Sun resides in this constellation at that time. Calendars that begin January 1 circulate energy from both Sirius and Vega, since the Sun aligns with those two stars at that time. It is helpful to recognize that all calendars, including the Maya calendar, are practical applications of astrology.

LONG COUNT

Another component of the Maya calendar is called the Long Count. It is made up of the larger cycles of the Maya calendar and seems to extend to infinity. It is composed of a 360-day cycle called *tun*, a 20-tun cycle called *katun* and a 20-katun (400-tun) cycle called *baktun*. There are also larger cycles calculated by multiplying the baktun by twenty, the resulting cycle by twenty and so on.

In the astrological use of the Long Count, a 13-tun cycle, a 13-katun cycle and a 13-baktun cycle are also counted. Notice the similarity between the 360 days of the tun and the 360° of a circle and the zodiac. Don't confuse the 360-day tun with the 365-day Haab. The 360-day tun is composed of complete 20-day Daykeeper cycles (18 x 20 = 360), while the 365-day Haab is not.

tun	360 days	1 tun	nearly a year
13-tun	4680 days	13 tun	12.8 years
katun	7200 days	20 tun	19.7 years
13-katun	93,600 days	260 tun	256+ years
baktun	144,000 days	400 tun	394+ years
13-baktun	1,872,000 days	5200 tun	5125+ years

What is relevant to us today is that we are approaching the end of a 13-baktun cycle. When people say that the Maya calendar ends in 2012, they are referring to the end of this 5125-year cycle that began in 3114 BCE. There is some controversy over the starting and ending dates of this particular 13-baktun cycle.

In order to better understand why some believe that the Maya Long Count actually ends in 2012, it is necessary to recognize certain astrological and galactic cycles. There exist astrological cycles that map the "light" of creation, the "seedings" from the darkness and the interplay between the light and the dark that is fundamental to creation itself. The cycles of the Sun and Venus together are a key *light* cycle. Eclipse cycles are a fundamental cycle of *darkness* for the Earth. The interrelationships between the cycles of light and dark reveal the ongoing creation of life on the Earth and the evolution of the Earth within the Galaxy.

A major Sun/Venus event occurs in 2012, as do two profound solar eclipses. The coming together of a *cycle of light* and a *cycle of darkness* at the time of the conclusion of a unique series of galactic alignments hints at the underlying reason why the conclusion of this Maya 13-baktun cycle is sometimes called the end of the Maya calendar.

In 2012 there will be the rare occurrence of a *transit of Venus*. This is when Venus passes directly in front of the Sun from our perspective on the Earth. It is a perfect alignment between the Earth, Venus and the Sun. The last transit of Venus occurred in 1882, around the time of the rediscovery of ancient Maya sacred sites. Transits of Venus occur on the average twice every 120 or so years.

Two solar eclipses happen in 2012. One takes place with the Sun and Moon aligned with, and astrologically conjunct, the Pleiades. The other solar eclipse, later that same year, has the Sun and the Moon aligned with the head of the constellation of Serpens, the Serpent. The Pleiades and the Serpent are essential keys in Maya astrology.

The winter solstice of 2012 is the last in a series of solstices that have the Sun's disk precisely aligned with the equator of our Galaxy, commonly called the Milky Way. These alignments began around the time of Harmonic Convergence in 1987. The solstices from 1998 through 2001 have the *center of the Sun* exactly aligned with *the center of the galactic equator!*

In 2012 there will be unique celestial alignments involving the Sun, the Moon, the Earth, Venus, the Pleiades, the Serpent and the Galaxy. These are all considered within advanced Maya astrology. ★

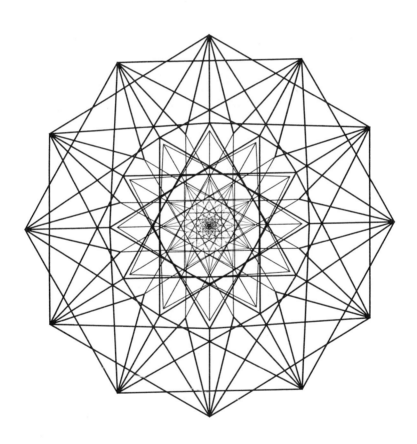

GALACTIC TIMING

The Sun and all the stars seen in the night sky are living entities within the form of the Milky Way Galaxy. They can be seen as cells in the body of the Galaxy, analogous to the billions of cells that make up the human body. The center of the Galaxy is like the human heart: they both regulate circulation throughout the body. All the stars in our area of space, including the Sun, are affected by what is happening with the Galaxy, since they make up a part of its body.

There is something happening in the heavens that has never occurred in the history of human civilization. There is a unique alignment currently under way involving our Earth, our Sun and our Galaxy. The present alignment suggests that the Earth is beginning to receive energy and information more directly from the Galactic Center. It is like we are being directly plugged into a galactic "outlet" or energy source. The rapid changes and transformations occurring at this time can be attributed to this influx of higher frequencies.

The spring and autumn equinoxes and the summer and winter solstices mark the beginning of the four seasons. To many people on the Earth, these are sacred times that are celebrated in a variety of ways. Even in the modern Christian tradition, the major holidays of Easter and Christmas are in close proximity to the spring equinox and winter solstice, respectively. What occurs at these four sacred moments is an influx of spiritual and archetypal energy from the stars to the Earth. The winter solstice takes on great, although mostly unconscious, cultural significance for us due to its taking place during the holiday season and near the time of our new year. It is the winter solstice that is currently making the galactic connection.

If you look up at the sky on a dark, clear night you can see the cloudy band of stars called the Milky Way. This high concentration of stars is due to their lying along the equator of our Galaxy. (See next graphic.)

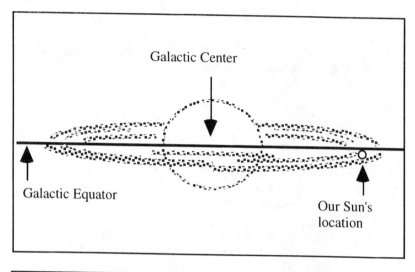

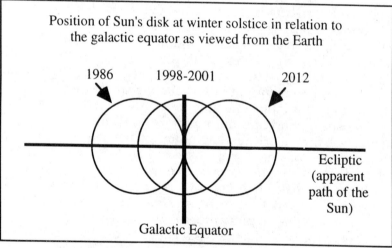

At the moment of the twenty-six winter solstices from 1986 through 2012, the Sun's disk is aligned with the center of this Milky Way band of stars, technically referred to as the galactic equator. If we could see the Sun and the stars at the same time, we could see that the Sun is in the middle of this cloudy band of stars near the Galactic Center at the moment of the winter solstice.

This suggests that in addition to the spiritual and archetypal energies that come to the Earth from the stars at the moment of the solstice, there is also a higher level of galactic input. The *center* of the Sun's disk, when viewed from the Earth, is precisely aligned with the center line of the Milky Way or galactic equator at the 1998 winter solstice and all solstices through the summer solstice 2001.

This series of galactic alignments will conclude at the 2012 winter solstice, which is also the end of a 5125-year-long, 13-baktun Maya calendar cycle. This twenty-six-year period, from 1986 through 2012, correlates with the last two 13-tun cycles in this concluding 13-baktun cycle. The last time the solstices aligned with the galactic equator was 13,000 years ago.

The Maya calendar tracks cycles from a galactic level. This includes multidimensional realities that extend beyond the boundary of our solar system. As we investigate and understand more of our relationship to the Galaxy we live in, more of the Maya calendar's potential can reveal itself to us.

Our present time and the early 23rd century have something unique in common – both have galactic alignments. Our time has the winter solstice Sun aligning with the *equator* of our Galaxy, but in the future, the winter solstice Sun will be aligning with the actual *center* of our Galaxy.

To stimulate your imagination, consider that the 23rd century is the time period of the earliest *Star Trek* adventures. Consider that in *Star Trek*, they have intragalactic star travel and interactions with our galactic neighbors. Many episodes of *Star Trek* begin with the captain saying, "Captain's log, stardate . . ." This stardate chronology also begins early in the 23rd century at the time of the solstice/galactic center alignment! This stardate count is galactic in the sense that it is not limited to a single planet or solar system. It works throughout the galaxy. Those who have been initiated into the Tzol'Kin realize that the Maya calendar is also based on galactic time and is not limited to our planet or solar system.

One galactic alignment (1986-2012) concludes with the end of a Maya calendar cycle and the other takes place at the end of the 6000-year biblical cycle (2240). In the Bible, on the fourth day of creation, G-d said, "Let there be lights in the expanse of the sky to separate day from night; they shall serve as signs for the set times – the days and the years; and they shall serve as lights in the expanse of the sky to shine upon the Earth." And G-d saw how good this was.

As the whole of humanity comes together in a new and globally conscious way, maybe it is time to open up to the gifts that each culture on the Earth has to offer us. This will assist us in healing ourselves and bringing people together with mutual respect and love for each other. The Maya key to understanding and attuning to galactic cycles of time is offered to those who choose to open their hearts, take full responsibility for all their experiences and expand beyond the limitations of the ego into time beyond time. ★

FOLLOWING THE MAYA CALENDAR

What is known about the Maya calendar is that it is composed of a variety of interrelated cycles. Being aware of the movement of the twenty Daykeepers provides access to a galactic level of the Maya calendar. It is at this level that most of the cycles associated with the Maya calendar find a common source. To experience the Maya calendar as a holistic and integrated system, it is necessary to consciously maintain an awareness of the galactic level.

TZOL'KIN

The appearance and presence of each of the twenty Daykeepers, one on each day for twenty consecutive days, can be experienced as an ever-repeating twenty-day cycle. Combining this twenty-day cycle with a thirteen-day cycle, matching each Daykeeper with a number from one to thirteen over a period of 260 days, is the basic pattern of the Tzol'Kin.

Only by maintaining an awareness of the Tzol'Kin while you follow or consider other cycles of the Maya calendar, does the calendar offer access to levels of consciousness beyond that of normal ego-centered reality. It is beyond the ego that you find the path in consciousness mapped out by the Maya calendar.

To follow the pattern of a Tzol'Kin cycle, we'll start with the number 1 and the Daykeeper Imix. (See the following table.) The next day, day #2, has the number 2 and the Daykeeper Ik. This matching of number and Daykeeper continues through the thirteenth day with the number 13 and Ben as Daykeeper. This day completes a 13-day cycle. The next day, day #14, starts a new 13-day cycle with a number 1 along with the Daykeeper Ix. We continue on to the twentieth day, with the number 7 and Ahaw as Daykeeper. This day completes a 20-day cycle of the Daykeepers.

The next day, day #21, has Imix as Daykeeper, the same as twenty days earlier on day #1. We can see that day #26 completes another 13-day cycle, so the next day has the number 1 with the Daykeeper Manik. This pattern continues for the 260-day cycle, where each of the twenty Daykeepers has been combined with each of thirteen numbers.

Day #1	Day #2	Day #3	Day #4	Day #5
1 Imix	**2 Ik**	3 Ak'bal	4 K'an	5 Chik'chan
Day #6	Day #7	Day #8	Day #9	Day #10
6 Kimi	7 Manik	8 Lamat	9 Muluk	10 Ok
Day #11	Day #12	**Day #13**	**Day #14**	Day #15
11 Chuen	12 Eb	**13 Ben**	**1 Ix**	2 Men
Day #16	Day #17	Day #18	Day #19	**Day #20**
3 Kib	4 Kaban	5 Etz'nab	6 Kawak	**7 Ahaw**
Day #21	Day #22	Day #23	Day #24	Day #25
8 Imix.	9 Ix	10 Ak'bal	11 K'an	12 Chik'chan
Day #26	**Day #27**	Day #28	Day #29	Day #30 ...
13 Kimi	**1 Manik**	2 Lamat	3 Muluk	4 Ok ...

The Tzol'Kin is a perpetual 260-day cycle and doesn't have a natural beginning or an end. A Tzol'Kin cycle can be counted from any day in the Tzol'Kin, through 260 days, until the return of the same Tzol'Kin day that was chosen as the starting day.

In addition to the Traditional Tzol'Kin count, another Tzol'Kin was revealed around the time of Harmonic Convergence in 1987. This we call the New Age Tzol'Kin count. The Traditional count and the New Age are different in that they match different Tzol'Kin days with any given day. For example, August 16, 1987, was a 1-Imix in the Traditional count and simultaneously a 3-Men in the New Age count.

The following table gives the dates for successive 4-Ahaw days in the Traditional Tzol'Kin count along with the corresponding day in the New Age Tzol'Kin count. The numbers in ( ) indicate where the day is in a 260-day cycle, assuming 1-Imix as day (1) and 13-Ahaw as day (260). These numbers serve as aids to certain calculations and do not imply that the cycle actual begins on day (1) and ends on day (260).

Traditional 4-Ahaw (160)	New Age Day-Sign
January 9, 1998	3-Chuen (211)
September 26, 1998	3-Chuen (211)
June 13, 1999	3-Chuen (211)
February 28, 2000	3-Chuen (211)
November 14, 2000	2-Ok (210)
August 1, 2001	2-Ok (210)
April 18, 2002	2-Ok (210)
January 3, 2003	2-Ok (210)
September 20, 2003	2-Ok (210)
June 6, 2004	1-Muluk (209)
February 21, 2005	1-Muluk (209)
November 8, 2005	1-Muluk (209)
July 26, 2006	1-Muluk (209)
April 12, 2007	1-Muluk (209)
December 28, 2007	1-Muluk (209)
September 13, 2008	13-Lamat (208)
May 31, 2009	13-Lamat (208)
February 15, 2010	13-Lamat (208)
November 2, 2010	13-Lamat (208)
July 20, 2011	13-Lamat (208)
April 5, 2012	12-Manik (207)
December 21, 2012	12-Manik (207)

Another significant difference between the Traditional and the New Age counts is that the New Age count skips Leap Day, February 29, every four years. The Traditional count doesn't skip this day, so the two Tzol'Kin counts shift one day in relationship to each other every four years on February 29. This can be seen in the previous table. The difference between the two counts from February 29, 1996, through February 28, 2000, is 51 days. Using the table, you can subtract 160 (4-Ahaw) from 211 (3-Chuen) to get 51. From February 29, 2000, through February 28, 2004, the difference is 50 days (210 - 160 = 50). From February 29, 2004, through February 28, 2008, the difference is 49 days (209 - 160 = 49). The changing relationship between the two Tzol'Kin counts suggests a possible larger *galactic* cycle.

TUN

There is another basic cycle in the Maya calendar that is based on the twenty-day Daykeeper cycle. Counting through eighteen of these twenty-day cycles reveals a larger cycle composed of 360 days (18 x 20 = 360). This cycle has the name tun (sounds like "tune"). Twenty tun make up a larger cycle, called katun.

The following table gives the ending dates for the tun in the current katun. The **bold** number in the third place, counting from the right, indicates how many tun have completed. Every tun ends on an Ahaw day. Which Ahaw day, according to the Traditional Tzol'Kin, is also included in this table.

April 10, 1992	10-Ahaw	12.18.**19**.0.0
April 5, 1993*	6-Ahaw	12.19.**0**.0.0
March 31, 1994	2-Ahaw	12.19.**1**.0.0
March 26, 1995	11-Ahaw	12.19.**2**.0.0
March 20, 1996	7-Ahaw	12.19.**3**.0.0
March 15, 1997	3-Ahaw	12.19.**4**.0.0
March 10, 1998	12-Ahaw	12.19.**5**.0.0
March 5, 1999	8-Ahaw	12.19.**6**.0.0
February 28, 2000*	4-Ahaw	12.19.**7**.0.0
February 22, 2001	13-Ahaw	12.19.**8**.0.0
February 17, 2002	9-Ahaw	12.19.**9**.0.0
February 12, 2003	5-Ahaw	12.19.**10**.0.0
February 7, 2004	1-Ahaw	12.19.**11**.0.0
February 1, 2005	10-Ahaw	12.19.**12**.0.0
January 27, 2006	6-Ahaw	12.19.**13**.0.0
January 22, 2007	2-Ahaw	12.19.**14**.0.0
January 17, 2008	11-Ahaw	12.19.**15**.0.0
January 11, 2009	7-Ahaw	12.19.**16**.0.0
January 6, 2010	3-Ahaw	12.19.**17**.0.0
January 1, 2011	12-Ahaw	12.19.**18**.0.0
December 27, 2011	8-Ahaw	12.19.**19**.0.0
December 21, 2012*	4-Ahaw	13.0.**0**.0.0

Note: Dates in the Maya calendar can be identified using a five-place notation system as found in the previous table and also the following tables in this chapter. The place to the far right counts single days from 0 to 19. The next place counts twenty-day periods from 0 to 18. The third place from the right counts tun from 0 to 19. The fourth place counts baktun from 0 to 19 and the fifth place counts baktun.

For example, February 28, 2000, has a Maya date of 12.19.7.0.0. This indicates that twelve (12) baktun, nineteen (19) katun, seven (7) tun, zero (0) 20-day periods and zero (0) days have passed since the start of the count in 3114 BCE.

For December 21, 2012, the date is 13.0.0.0.0. Thirteen tun cycles complete between 12.19.7.0.0 and 13.0.0.0.0. Adding thirteen tun to the seven from the earlier date brings the tun count to twenty. This is the same as one katun. Adding the one katun to the nineteen katun from the earlier date gives twenty katun, or one baktun. Adding one baktun to the earlier twelve makes it thirteen baktun with zeros for all the other places.

13-TUN

A special day in the previous table is February 28, 2000, 4-Ahaw. This day concludes a 13-tun cycle. The next day, February 29, 2000, is a millennial Leap Day and starts the final 13-tun. The 13-tun cycles are galactic, since they have the capacity to *carry* complete Tzol'Kin cycles. 13 x 360 days = 4680 days. 18 x 260 days = 4680 days.

February 4, 1936	4-Ahaw	12.16.2.0.0
November 27, 1948	4-Ahaw	12.16.15.0.0
September 20, 1961	4-Ahaw	12.17.8.0.0
July 14, 1974	4-Ahaw	12.18.1.0.0
May 7, 1987	4-Ahaw	12.18.14.0.0
February 28, 2000	4-Ahaw	12.19.7.0.0
December 21, 2012	4-Ahaw	13.0.0.0.0

Ending dates for recent 13-tun cycles.

KATUN

The katun cycle is composed of twenty tun cycles. Each katun is composed of 7200 days (20 x 360 = 7200) and lasts about 19.7 of our years.

Twenty katun cycles make up a baktun cycle. The nineteenth (19) katun of the current baktun ended April 5, 1993. (See the earlier table under **Tun**.) The twentieth and last katun of the current baktun ends on December 21, 2012. In Maya calendar notation for December 21, 2012, the fourth place from the right has a zero indicating the completion of the twentieth katun, which in turn concludes the thirteenth baktun as shown by the thirteen (13) in the next place to the far left.

13-KATUN

Thirteen katun cycles are considered as a galactic cycle, since they are divisible by complete Tzol'Kin cycles. A 13-katun lasts a bit over 256 of our years. The 93,600 days in a 13-katun cycle carries within it 360 Tzol'Kin (360 x 260 = 93,600). A 13-katun cycle can also be seen as 260-tun.

February 24, 1244	4-Ahaw	11.1.0.0.0
May 30, 1500	4-Ahaw	11.14.0.0.0
September 14, 1756	4-Ahaw	12.7.0.0.0
December 21, 2012	4-Ahaw	13.0.0.0.0

Ending dates for recent 13-katun cycles.

BAKTUN

A baktun is made up of twenty katun cycles. It lasts for 144,000 days and a little over 394 of our years. The current baktun began September 18, 1618, and concludes December 21, 2012.

13-BAKTUN

The current baktun is the thirteenth in a series of thirteen that began in 3114 BCE. The 13-baktun cycle is another galactic cycle, due to its capacity to carry complete Tzol'Kin cycles.

It is composed of 1,872,000 days. 7200 Tzol'Kin will be complete, counting from the beginning of the 13-baktun cycle that began about 5125 years ago, to its conclusion on December 21, 2012. A 13-baktun cycle also contains 260-katun. The ending of this current 13-baktun cycle is sometimes referred to as the end of the Maya calendar.

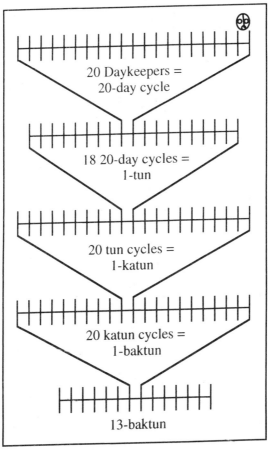

20 Daykeepers = 20-day cycle

18 20-day cycles = 1-tun

20 tun cycles = 1-katun

20 katun cycles = 1-baktun

13-baktun

The pattern of the Maya Long Count is illustrated above. The Daykeepers create a 20-day cycle. Eighteen of these 20-day cycles constitutes a tun cycle. Twenty tun cycles compose a katun cycle and twenty katun make up a baktun. A 13-baktun cycle is composed of 13 baktun, 260 katun, 5200 tun, 93,600 20-day-long Daykeeper cycles or 1,872,000 days. ★

MAYA CALENDAR DATES

Chronological listing of important dates from the previous chapter.
(Starting in 1998 through the end of 2012.)

Modern Date	Traditional Tzol'Kin	Maya Long Count
January 9, 1998	4-Ahaw	12.19.4.15.0
March 10, 1998	12-Ahaw	12.19.5.0.0
September 26, 1998	4-Ahaw	12.19.5.10.0
March 5, 1999	8-Ahaw	12.19.6.0.0
June 13, 1999	4-Ahaw	12.19.6.5.0
February 28, 2000	4-Ahaw	12.19.7.0.0
November 14, 2000	4-Ahaw	12.19.7.13.0
February 22, 2001	13-Ahaw	12.19.8.0.0
August 1, 2001	4-Ahaw	12.19.8.8.0
February 17, 2002	9-Ahaw	12.19.9.0.0
April 18, 2002	4-Ahaw	12.19.9.3.0
January 3, 2003	4-Ahaw	12.19.9.19.0
February 12, 2003	5-Ahaw	12.19.10.0.0
September 20, 2003	4-Ahaw	12.19.10.11.0
February 7, 2004	1-Ahaw	12.19.11.0.0
June 6, 2004	4-Ahaw	12.19.11.6.0
February 1, 2005	10-Ahaw	12.19.12.0.0
February 21, 2005	4-Ahaw	12.19.12.1.0
November 8, 2005	4-Ahaw	12.19.12.14.0
January 27, 2006	6-Ahaw	12.19.13.0.0
July 26, 2006	4-Ahaw	12.19.13.9.0
January 22, 2007	2-Ahaw	12.19.14.0.0
April 12, 2007	4-Ahaw	12.19.14.4.0
December 28, 2007	4-Ahaw	12.19.14.17.0
January 17, 2008	11-Ahaw	12.19.15.0.0
September 13, 2008	4-Ahaw	12.19.15.12.0
January 11, 2009	7-Ahaw	12.19.16.0.0
May 31, 2009	4-Ahaw	12.19.16.7.0
January 6, 2010	3-Ahaw	12.19.17.0.0
February 15, 2010	4-Ahaw	12.19.17.2.0
November 2, 2010	4-Ahaw	12.19.17.15.0
January 1, 2011	12-Ahaw	12.19.18.0.0
July 20, 2011	4-Ahaw	12.19.18.10.0
December 27, 2011	8-Ahaw	12.19.19.0.0
April 5, 2012	4-Ahaw	12.19.19.5.0
December 21, 2012	4-Ahaw	13.0.0.0.0

DAYKEEPER FINDER

INSTRUCTIONS

Follow these easy steps to find the Daykeeper for any day in the modern calendar. The following tables work for the New Age Tzol'Kin count. To find the Daykeeper according to the Traditional Tzol'Kin, first find the Daykeeper in these tables and then go to the **New to Old Conversion Table** that follows these tables.

STEP 1.

First find the year of the date that you are converting at the top of one of the four tables on the following pages.

STEP 2.

In the table that has the correct year for the date in question, look to find the month along the top and the day along the left side of the table. Find where these meet within the table to find the Daykeeper for that day. If the time of day was after sunset, but before midnight, then go to the Daykeeper for the next day. This is because the Daykeepers change at sunset.

NOTE:

You may wonder why the **Daykeeper Finder** tables are for the New Age Tzol'Kin count and not for the Traditional Tzol'Kin count. The reason they are set up this way is for convenience, simplicity and to minimize the amount of space used for the following tables. It does not in any way suggest a preference for either count.

DAYKEEPER FINDER - TABLE 1

For the New Age Tzol'Kin during the following years:

... 1878, 1882, 1886, 1890, 1894, 1898, 1902, 1906, 1910, 1914, 1918,
1922, 1926, 1930, 1934, 1938, 1942, 1946, 1950, 1954, 1958, 1962, 1966,
1970, 1974, 1978, 1982, 1986, 1990, 1994, 1998, 2002, 2006, 2010, ...

	Jan/May	Feb/Jun	March	April	July	August	Sept.	October	Nov.	Dec.
1	Akbal	Ix	Ik	Ben	Kan	Men	Kimi	Kib	Manik	Kaban
2	Kan	Men	Akbal	Ix	Chikchan	Kib	Manik	Kaban	Lamat	Etznab
3	Chikchan	Kib	Kan	Men	Kimi	Kaban	Lamat	Etznab	Muluk	Kawak
4	Kimi	Kaban	Chikchan	Kib	Manik	Etznab	Muluk	Kawak	Ok	Ahaw
5	Manik	Etznab	Kimi	Kaban	Lamat	Kawak	Ok	Ahaw	Chuen	Imix
6	Lamat	Kawak	Manik	Etznab	Muluk	Ahaw	Chuen	Imix	Eb	Ik
7	Muluk	Ahaw	Lamat	Kawak	Ok	Imix	Eb	Ik	Ben	Akbal
8	Ok	Imix	Muluk	Ahaw	Chuen	Ik	Ben	Akbal	Ix	Kan
9	Chuen	Ik	Ok	Imix	Eb	Akbal	Ix	Kan	Men	Chikchan
10	Eb	Akbal	Chuen	Ik	Ben	Kan	Men	Chikchan	Kib	Kimi
11	Ben	Kan	Eb	Akbal	Ix	Chikchan	Kib	Kimi	Kaban	Manik
12	Ix	Chikchan	Ben	Kan	Men	Kimi	Kaban	Manik	Etznab	Lamat
13	Men	Kimi	Ix	Chikchan	Kib	Manik	Etznab	Lamat	Kawak	Muluk
14	Kib	Manik	Men	Kimi	Kaban	Lamat	Kawak	Muluk	Ahaw	Ok
15	Kaban	Lamat	Kib	Manik	Etznab	Muluk	Ahaw	Ok	Imix	Chuen
16	Etznab	Muluk	Kaban	Lamat	Kawak	Ok	Imix	Chuen	Ik	Eb
17	Kawak	Ok	Etznab	Muluk	Ahaw	Chuen	Ik	Eb	Akbal	Ben
18	Ahaw	Chuen	Kawak	Ok	Imix	Eb	Akbal	Ben	Kan	Ix
19	Imix	Eb	Ahaw	Chuen	Ik	Ben	Kan	Ix	Chikchan	Men
20	Ik	Ben	Imix	Eb	Akbal	Ix	Chikchan	Men	Kimi	Kib
21	Akbal	Ix	Ik	Ben	Kan	Men	Kimi	Kib	Manik	Kaban
22	Kan	Men	Akbal	Ix	Chikchan	Kib	Manik	Kaban	Lamat	Etznab
23	Chikchan	Kib	Kan	Men	Kimi	Kaban	Lamat	Etznab	Muluk	Kawak
24	Kimi	Kaban	Chikchan	Kib	Manik	Etznab	Muluk	Kawak	Ok	Ahaw
25	Manik	Etznab	Kimi	Kaban	Lamat	Kawak	Ok	Ahaw	Chuen	Imix
26	Lamat	Kawak	Manik	Etznab	Muluk	Ahaw	Chuen	Imix	Eb	Ik
27	Muluk	Ahaw	Lamat	Kawak	Ok	Imix	Eb	Ik	Ben	Akbal
28	Ok	Imix	Muluk	Ahaw	Chuen	Ik	Ben	Akbal	Ix	Kan
29	Chuen	Ik	Ok	Imix	Eb	Akbal	Ix	Kan	Men	Chikchan
30	Eb	Akbal	Chuen	Ik	Ben	Kan	Men	Chikchan	Kib	Kimi
31	Ben		Eb		Ix	Chikchan		Kimi		Manik

DAYKEEPER FINDER - TABLE 2

For the New Age Tzol'Kin during the following years:

... 1879, 1883, 1887, 1891, 1895, 1899, 1903, 1907, 1911, 1915, 1919, 1923, 1927, 1931, 1935, 1939, 1943, 1947, 1951, 1955, 1959, 1963, 1967, 1971, 1975, 1979, 1983, 1987, 1991, 1995, 1999, 2003, 2007, 2011, ...

	Jan/May	Feb/Jun	March	April	July	August	Sept.	October	Nov.	Dec.
1	Lamat	Kawak	Manik	Etznab	Muluk	Ahaw	Chuen	Imix	Eb	Ik
2	Muluk	Ahaw	Lamat	Kawak	Ok	Imix	Eb	Ik	Ben	Akbal
3	Ok	Imix	Muluk	Ahaw	Chuen	Ik	Ben	Akbal	Ix	Kan
4	Chuen	Ik	Ok	Imix	Eb	Akbal	Ix	Kan	Men	Chikchan
5	Eb	Akbal	Chuen	Ik	Ben	Kan	Men	Chikchan	Kib	Kimi
6	Ben	Kan	Eb	Akbal	Ix	Chikchan	Kib	Kimi	Kaban	Manik
7	Ix	Chikchan	Ben	Kan	Men	Kimi	Kaban	Manik	Etznab	Lamat
8	Men	Kimi	Ix	Chikchan	Kib	Manik	Etznab	Lamat	Kawak	Muluk
9	Kib	Manik	Men	Kimi	Kaban	Lamat	Kawak	Muluk	Ahaw	Ok
10	Kaban	Lamat	Kib	Manik	Etznab	Muluk	Ahaw	Ok	Imix	Chuen
11	Etznab	Muluk	Kaban	Lamat	Kawak	Ok	Imix	Chuen	Ik	Eb
12	Kawak	Ok	Etznab	Muluk	Ahaw	Chuen	Ik	Eb	Akbal	Ben
13	Ahaw	Chuen	Kawak	Ok	Imix	Eb	Akbal	Ben	Kan	Ix
14	Imix	Eb	Ahaw	Chuen	Ik	Ben	Kan	Ix	Chikchan	Men
15	Ik	Ben	Imix	Eb	Akbal	Ix	Chikchan	Men	Kimi	Kib
16	Akbal	Ix	Ik	Ben	Kan	Men	Kimi	Kib	Manik	Kaban
17	Kan	Men	Akbal	Ix	Chikchan	Kib	Manik	Kaban	Lamat	Etznab
18	Chikchan	Kib	Kan	Men	Kimi	Kaban	Lamat	Etznab	Muluk	Kawak
19	Kimi	Kaban	Chikchan	Kib	Manik	Etznab	Muluk	Kawak	Ok	Ahaw
20	Manik	Etznab	Kimi	Kaban	Lamat	Kawak	Ok	Ahaw	Chuen	Imix
21	Lamat	Kawak	Manik	Etznab	Muluk	Ahaw	Chuen	Imix	Eb	Ik
22	Muluk	Ahaw	Lamat	Kawak	Ok	Imix	Eb	Ik	Ben	Akbal
23	Ok	Imix	Muluk	Ahaw	Chuen	Ik	Ben	Akbal	Ix	Kan
24	Chuen	Ik	Ok	Imix	Eb	Akbal	Ix	Kan	Men	Chikchan
25	Eb	Akbal	Chuen	Ik	Ben	Kan	Men	Chikchan	Kib	Kimi
26	Ben	Kan	Eb	Akbal	Ix	Chikchan	Kib	Kimi	Kaban	Manik
27	Ix	Chikchan	Ben	Kan	Men	Kimi	Kaban	Manik	Etznab	Lamat
28	Men	Kimi	Ix	Chikchan	Kib	Manik	Etznab	Lamat	Kawak	Muluk
29	Kib	Manik	Men	Kimi	Kaban	Lamat	Kawak	Muluk	Ahaw	Ok
30	Kaban	Lamat	Kib	Manik	Etznab	Muluk	Ahaw	Ok	Imix	Chuen
31	Etznab		Kaban		Kawak	Ok		Chuen		Eb

DAYKEEPER FINDER - TABLE 3

For the New Age Tzol'Kin during the following years:
... 1880, 1884, 1888, 1892, 1896, 1900, 1904, 1908, 1912, 1916, 1920,
1924, 1928, 1932, 1936, 1940, 1944, 1948, 1952, 1956, 1960, 1964, 1968,
1972, 1976, 1980, 1984, 1988, 1992, 1996, 2000, 2004, 2008, 2012, ...

	Jan/May	Feb/Jun	March	April	July	August	Sept.	October	Nov.	Dec.
1	Ben	Kan	Eb	Akbal	Ix	Chikchan	Kib	Kimi	Kaban	Manik
2	Ix	Chikchan	Ben	Kan	Men	Kimi	Kaban	Manik	Etznab	Lamat
3	Men	Kimi	Ix	Chikchan	Kib	Manik	Etznab	Lamat	Kawak	Muluk
4	Kib	Manik	Men	Kimi	Kaban	Lamat	Kawak	Muluk	Ahaw	Ok
5	Kaban	Lamat	Kib	Manik	Etznab	Muluk	Ahaw	Ok	Imix	Chuen
6	Etznab	Muluk	Kaban	Lamat	Kawak	Ok	Imix	Chuen	Ik	Eb
7	Kawak	Ok	Etznab	Muluk	Ahaw	Chuen	Ik	Eb	Akbal	Ben
8	Ahaw	Chuen	Kawak	Ok	Imix	Eb	Akbal	Ben	Kan	Ix
9	Imix	Eb	Ahaw	Chuen	Ik	Ben	Kan	Ix	Chikchan	Men
10	Ik	Ben	Imix	Eb	Akbal	Ix	Chikchan	Men	Kimi	Kib
11	Akbal	Ix	Ik	Ben	Kan	Men	Kimi	Kib	Manik	Kaban
12	Kan	Men	Akbal	Ix	Chikchan	Kib	Manik	Kaban	Lamat	Etznab
13	Chikchan	Kib	Kan	Men	Kimi	Kaban	Lamat	Etznab	Muluk	Kawak
14	Kimi	Kaban	Chikchan	Kib	Manik	Etznab	Muluk	Kawak	Ok	Ahaw
15	Manik	Etznab	Kimi	Kaban	Lamat	Kawak	Ok	Ahaw	Chuen	Imix
16	Lamat	Kawak	Manik	Etznab	Muluk	Ahaw	Chuen	Imix	Eb	Ik
17	Muluk	Ahaw	Lamat	Kawak	Ok	Imix	Eb	Ik	Ben	Akbal
18	Ok	Imix	Muluk	Ahaw	Chuen	Ik	Ben	Akbal	Ix	Kan
19	Chuen	Ik	Ok	Imix	Eb	Akbal	Ix	Kan	Men	Chikchan
20	Eb	Akbal	Chuen	Ik	Ben	Kan	Men	Chikchan	Kib	Kimi
21	Ben	Kan	Eb	Akbal	Ix	Chikchan	Kib	Kimi	Kaban	Manik
22	Ix	Chikchan	Ben	Kan	Men	Kimi	Kaban	Manik	Etznab	Lamat
23	Men	Kimi	Ix	Chikchan	Kib	Manik	Etznab	Lamat	Kawak	Muluk
24	Kib	Manik	Men	Kimi	Kaban	Lamat	Kawak	Muluk	Ahaw	Ok
25	Kaban	Lamat	Kib	Manik	Etznab	Muluk	Ahaw	Ok	Imix	Chuen
26	Etznab	Muluk	Kaban	Lamat	Kawak	Ok	Imix	Chuen	Ik	Eb
27	Kawak	Ok	Etznab	Muluk	Ahaw	Chuen	Ik	Eb	Akbal	Ben
28	Ahaw	Chuen	Kawak	Ok	Imix	Eb	Akbal	Ben	Kan	Ix
29	Imix	Eb	Ahaw	Chuen	Ik	Ben	Kan	Ix	Chikchan	Men
30	Ik	Ben	Imix	Eb	Akbal	Ix	Chikchan	Men	Kimi	Kib
31	Akbal		Ik		Kan	Men		Kib		Kaban

DAYKEEPER FINDER - TABLE 4

For the New Age Tzol'Kin during the following years:

.... 1881, 1885, 1889, 1893, 1897, 1901, 1905, 1909, 1913, 1917, 1921, 1925, 1929, 1933, 1937, 1941, 1945, 1949, 1953, 1957, 1961, 1965, 1969, 1973, 1977, 1981, 1985, 1989, 1993, 1997, 2001, 2005, 2009, 2013, ...

	Jan/May	Feb/Jun	March	April	July	August	Sept.	October	Nov.	Dec.
1	Etznab	Muluk	Kaban	Lamat	Kawak	Ok	Imix	Chuen	Ik	Eb
2	Kawak	Ok	Etznab	Muluk	Ahaw	Chuen	Ik	Eb	Akbal	Ben
3	Ahaw	Chuen	Kawak	Ok	Imix	Eb	Akbal	Ben	Kan	Ix
4	Imix	Eb	Ahaw	Chuen	Ik	Ben	Kan	Ix	Chikchan	Men
5	Ik	Ben	Imix	Eb	Akbal	Ix	Chikchan	Men	Kimi	Kib
6	Akbal	Ix	Ik	Ben	Kan	Men	Kimi	Kib	Manik	Kaban
7	Kan	Men	Akbal	Ix	Chikchan	Kib	Manik	Kaban	Lamat	Etznab
8	Chikchan	Kib	Kan	Men	Kimi	Kaban	Lamat	Etznab	Muluk	Kawak
9	Kimi	Kaban	Chikchan	Kib	Manik	Etznab	Muluk	Kawak	Ok	Ahaw
10	Manik	Etznab	Kimi	Kaban	Lamat	Kawak	Ok	Ahaw	Chuen	Imix
11	Lamat	Kawak	Manik	Etznab	Muluk	Ahaw	Chuen	Imix	Eb	Ik
12	Muluk	Ahaw	Lamat	Kawak	Ok	Imix	Eb	Ik	Ben	Akbal
13	Ok	Imix	Muluk	Ahaw	Chuen	Ik	Ben	Akbal	Ix	Kan
14	Chuen	Ik	Ok	Imix	Eb	Akbal	Ix	Kan	Men	Chikchan
15	Eb	Akbal	Chuen	Ik	Ben	Kan	Men	Chikchan	Kib	Kimi
16	Ben	Kan	Eb	Akbal	Ix	Chikchan	Kib	Kimi	Kaban	Manik
17	Ix	Chikchan	Ben	Kan	Men	Kimi	Kaban	Manik	Etznab	Lamat
18	Men	Kimi	Ix	Chikchan	Kib	Manik	Etznab	Lamat	Kawak	Muluk
19	Kib	Manik	Men	Kimi	Kaban	Lamat	Kawak	Muluk	Ahaw	Ok
20	Kaban	Lamat	Kib	Manik	Etznab	Muluk	Ahaw	Ok	Imix	Chuen
21	Etznab	Muluk	Kaban	Lamat	Kawak	Ok	Imix	Chuen	Ik	Eb
22	Kawak	Ok	Etznab	Muluk	Ahaw	Chuen	Ik	Eb	Akbal	Ben
23	Ahaw	Chuen	Kawak	Ok	Imix	Eb	Akbal	Ben	Kan	Ix
24	Imix	Eb	Ahaw	Chuen	Ik	Ben	Kan	Ix	Chikchan	Men
25	Ik	Ben	Imix	Eb	Akbal	Ix	Chikchan	Men	Kimi	Kib
26	Akbal	Ix	Ik	Ben	Kan	Men	Kimi	Kib	Manik	Kaban
27	Kan	Men	Akbal	Ix	Chikchan	Kib	Manik	Kaban	Lamat	Etznab
28	Chikchan	Kib	Kan	Men	Kimi	Kaban	Lamat	Etznab	Muluk	Kawak
29	Kimi	Kaban	Chikchan	Kib	Manik	Etznab	Muluk	Kawak	Ok	Ahaw
30	Manik	Etznab	Kimi	Kaban	Lamat	Kawak	Ok	Ahaw	Chuen	Imix
31	Lamat		Manik		Muluk	Ahaw		Imix		Ik

NEW TO OLD TABLE

Convert the New Age Tzol'Kin to the Traditional Tzol'Kin

INSTRUCTIONS

STEP 1: In the table on the facing page, first find the time frame for the date you are converting from the New Age Tzol'Kin to the Traditional Tzol'Kin.

STEP 2: Follow this row to the far right to find the number of Daykeepers needed to add to, or subtract from, the New Age Tzol'Kin Daykeeper to make the conversion. (For example, subtracting one may be easier than adding and counting nineteen.)

STEP 3: Use this number to count Daykeepers, starting with the New Age Tzol'Kin Daykeeper. To count, use the Counting Dial below the table or count inside the **Daykeeper Finder Tables**.
(Important: If using the **Daykeeper Finder Tables** to count, do not go from the Feb/June column into the March column or vice versa, from the June column back into the Feb/May column. Counting from the Feb/May column into the June column and vice versa is okay.)

Example: August 16, 1987, has Men as the Daykeeper (New Age), as can be found in the **Daykeeper Finder Tables**. In the following **New to Old** table, 1987 is between February 29, 1984, and February 28, 1988. Six (6) Daykeepers are needed to be added, as shown in the column to the far right. Counting clockwise from Men, Kib is one, Kaban is two, Etz'nab is three, Kawak is four, Ahaw is five and Imix is six. Imix is the Daykeeper according to the Traditional Tzol'Kin.

1876 through 1960	1960 through 2040	+	-
Feb. 29, 1876 through Feb. 28, 1880	Feb. 29, 1960 through Feb. 28, 1964	0	0
Feb. 29, 1880 through Feb. 28, 1884	Feb. 29, 1964 through Feb. 28, 1968	1	19
Feb. 29, 1884 through Feb. 28, 1888	Feb. 29, 1968 through Feb. 28, 1972	2	18
Feb. 29, 1888 through Feb. 28, 1892	Feb. 29, 1972 through Feb. 28, 1976	3	17
Feb. 29, 1892 through Feb. 28, 1896	Feb. 29, 1976 through Feb. 28, 1980	4	16
Feb. 29, 1896 through Feb. 28, 1904	Feb. 29, 1980 through Feb. 28, 1984	5	15
Feb. 29, 1904 through Feb. 28, 1908	Feb. 29, 1984 through Feb. 28, 1988	6	14
Feb. 29, 1908 through Feb. 28, 1912	Feb. 29, 1988 through Feb. 28, 1992	7	13
Feb. 29, 1912 through Feb. 28, 1916	Feb. 29, 1992 through Feb. 28, 1996	8	12
Feb. 29, 1916 through Feb. 28, 1920	Feb. 29, 1996 through Feb. 28, 2000	9	11
Feb. 29, 1920 through Feb. 28, 1924	Feb. 29, 2000 through Feb. 28, 2004	10	10
Feb. 29, 1924 through Feb. 28, 1928	Feb. 29, 2004 through Feb. 28, 2008	11	9
Feb. 29, 1928 through Feb. 28, 1932	Feb. 29, 2008 through Feb. 28, 2012	12	8
Feb. 29, 1932 through Feb. 28, 1936	Feb. 29, 2012 through Feb. 28, 2016	13	7
Feb. 29, 1936 through Feb. 28, 1940	Feb. 29, 2016 through Feb. 28, 2020	14	6
Feb. 29, 1940 through Feb. 28, 1944	Feb. 29, 2020 through Feb. 28, 2024	15	5
Feb. 29, 1944 through Feb. 28, 1948	Feb. 29, 2024 through Feb. 28, 2028	16	4
Feb. 29, 1948 through Feb. 28, 1952	Feb. 29, 2028 through Feb. 28, 2032	17	3
Feb. 29, 1952 through Feb. 28, 1956	Feb. 29, 2032 through Feb. 28, 2036	18	2
Feb. 29, 1956 through Feb. 28, 1960	Feb. 29, 2036 through Feb. 28, 2040	19	1

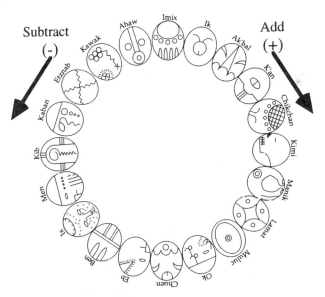

Subtract (-)   Add (+)

COUNTDOWN TO THE
END OF TIME

There are twenty Tzol'Kin cycles between September 27, 1998, and December 21, 2012. Each of these is guided by one of the twenty Daykeepers. The cycle from September 27, 1998, through June 13, 1999, is guided by Imix, the first Daykeeper. The second Daykeeper, Ik, is the guide for the next cycle, between June 14, 1999, and February 28, 2000. This pattern continues through the twentieth Tzol'Kin cycle, beginning on April 6, 2012, and ending on December 21, 2012. This completion cycle is guided by Ahaw, the Daykeeper who closes the "cycle of 20." ★

Start (5 Imix)	End (4 Ahaw)	Guide
September 27, 1998	June 13, 1999	Imix
June 14, 1999	February 28, 2000	Ik
February 29, 2000	November 14, 2000	Ak'bal
November 15, 2000	August 1, 2001	K'an
August 2, 2001	April 18, 2002	Chik'chan
April 19, 2002	January 3, 2003	Kimi
January 4, 2003	September 20, 2003	Manik
September 21, 2003	June 6, 2004	Lamat
June 7, 2004	February 21, 2005	Muluk
February 22, 2005	November 8, 2005	Ok
November 9, 2005	July 26, 2006	Chuen
July 27, 2006	April 12, 2007	Eb
April 13, 2007	December 28, 2007	Ben
December 29, 2007	September 13, 2008	Ix
September 14, 2008	May 31, 2009	Men
June 1, 2009	February 15, 2010	Kib
February 16, 2010	November 2, 2010	Kaban
November 3, 2010	July 20. 2011	Etz'nab
July 21, 2011	April 5, 2012	Kawak
April 6, 2012	December 21, 2012	Ahaw

EPILOGUE
FROM STACIA ALANA-LEAH

My first contact with the Maya calendar transformed my life into a spiritual adventure. The archetypes of the Daykeepers introduced themselves, one by one, and became my guides. Each Daykeeper has opened me to a completely new reality. They have given me a new taste of how multidimensional reality can be.

I have been exploring in an archetypal realm for many years, making it my goal to recognize the sacred within the mundane. Archetypes are the sacred presence that exists beyond time and space and beyond our personal experience. They appear in our reality similar to how movie images are projected from a reel of film. The personal light of our inner suns shines through them, focusing them before us. They are within, they are around, they are everywhere.

Realizing that archetypes are not the same as the brilliant light of my inner sun – in other words, my ego – was my first step in accessing reality beyond my personal experience. Just as we cannot fit an ocean of water into a small cup, we cannot fit all that we are into our egos. We can very easily pour the water from the cup into the ocean. We can also expand our consciousness into the vast domain of archetypal space, space beyond ego. From here we access multidimensional perception. Our consciousness is free and fluid, able to perceive things from many different perspectives. For in reality, we are everything and everything is us.

Meeting the archetypes of the Maya calendar was a very new experience for me. They tested and expanded my understanding of reality. They cleared a way for me to access a level of consciousness that I had not experienced before.

The Daykeepers took my understanding of archetypes to a new level. The rhythms of the cycles and the way they weave together came to life before my eyes and painted a vibrant tapestry of time as a multidimensional, living being. Needless to say, I was excited, overwhelmed and intrigued by this incredibly complex system known as the Maya calendar.

The archetypes of the Daykeepers, on the level we have accessed them, appear to be twenty different keys for perception. These twenty different keys are within each of us, some of them latent, some of them taken for granted and some of them overcompensating. Working with the twenty Daykeepers has enabled us to awaken and refine these inherent perceptive abilities. Each Daykeeper is a guide to awakening a new level of perception. They guide us through unknown, unexplainable territory that awakens our multidimensional understanding.

The Daykeepers continue to reveal more of who they are to us and continue to awaken deeper layers of our multidimensional abilities. They have revealed a nature of time that is alive and beautiful.

From our perspective, the path we are journeying on with the Daykeepers is an incredible gift and opportunity. Ray and I share the information contained in this book in the spirit of sharing a special gift. The gift is true time, the gift is alive. It is its nature to be freely given and to flow through our lives, bringing with it access to more of who we are. The journey is just beginning, the journey continues onward and the journey is complete. The gift is offered in each and every moment. ★